THE GUARDIAN TREE
The true story of Carmen Sylvia

THE GUARDIAN TREE
The true story of Carmen Sylvia (Revised 2016)

Written by: Laural Virtues Wauters
Cover Design: Anne Bronsveld & Bev Watkins
Edited by: Becky Lerner, Karla Giraldéz & Elizabeth Zack
Proofread by: Deb Kramer, Kristin Simons, Lara Drown, Maya Wauters,
Jean Wentz, Irmine Hero, Barbara and Steve Prust
Interior Design & Photography: Laural Virtues Wauters
Front Cover Photography: Laural Virtues Wauters
Back Cover Portrait: Kim Klein Photography
Publisher: Seven Earthly Virtues, LLC

LIBRARY OF CONGRESS CONTROL NUMBER: 2011938802

ISBN: 978-0-615-53459-6
Memoir, Spiritual Healing, Adoption

For more information, visit the author's website: **www.lauralwauters.com**

Other books written by Laural Virtues Wauters:
>   Tree Spirit Tarot – Return to the Garden of our Soul
>   Mandala Chakra – Awaken the One Within

TABLE OF CONTENTS

HOW DO I FEEL?

Like a rambling fool

A divine spirit

An inspired artist

A lonely child

A scared soul

A seeker of truth

A teacher for many

I have often described my life as a book I can't put down.

Since I was young I have known there are spirits in our lives who hold our book as we turn the pages.

I also believe that these spirits guide us as we experience the wonderful and difficult chapters of our lives.

This "knowing" has driven, confused and inspired me for over sixty years.

Now, the time has come for me to share what I have learned with you....

PROLOGUE: THE TREE

Deep within the fabled forests of Germania lived a sacred woodland grove. This primordial land was home to an ancient family of oak, chestnut and beech trees that nurtured humanity within its protective embrace.

In 768 Charlemagne, King of the Franks, chopped down several sacred oaks to force the conversion of Saxons to Christianity. He decreed that his Christian god was more powerful than their tree gods. Charlemagne named this place *Franconovurd* "Fjord of the Franks." Frankfurt grew into a powerful city for the Holy Roman Empire. In 1470 a wealthy patrician family named Holzhausen acquired land outside the city's north wall. They built a moated castle and surrounded it with a forested garden. In the 1500s Frankfurt was released from the Roman Empire's grip. As a "free city" it grew into Germany's financial center. The Holzhausen estate became known as *the Strange Land*. It was a safe haven for philosophers, artists and revolutionary thinkers to discuss concepts and radical ideas regarding religion, politics and human nature. In 1910 the last heir of the Holzhausen family gifted this special place to the city of Frankfurt to use as a public park. Its enchanted trees created a peaceful sanctuary for people of all ages. By 1955 most of Frankfurt's medieval city center had been destroyed by bombs and fires during WWII. Fortunately, Holzhausen Park and most of its trees survived.

In 1961 one of these wise old trees touched a young girl's soul. This encounter provided a lifetime of inspiration as the door to an epic adventure was about to open.

1

"One is wise to cultivate the tree
that bears fruit in our soul."
- Henry David Thoreau -

CHAPTER 1: THE FAIRY TALE

My first memories are filled with wonder as life around me often felt like a German fairy tale. I shared this magical adventure with my parents, John and Gertrude, my younger brother Henry, along with Tanta, Sisi and her husband Heinz. Plus, our Great Dane Gus.

We all lived in a seven-level villa near the entrance of Holzhausen Park. An avenue of graceful chestnut trees created a tunnel from our backyard to the park's front gate.

My parents had moved to Frankfurt from Wisconsin in 1948, as part of the Marshall Plan after WWII. My father worked in the IG Farben building a few blocks away, but he was often gone for weeks on end. When he was home, my father loved to sit in his favorite chair and drink German beer, while Gus, our great dane, lay on his lap like a giant pretzel. My father was a tall and gentle man with red hair and fair skin. His friends called him Rusty or Red. His smile reminded me of a Cheshire cat who knew much more than he wanted us to believe. I treasured my father for he made me feel safe.

From left to right - Gertrude, Henry, Laural and John standing on the landing leading up to the front door of our home.

3

My mother Gertrude was an extremely intense, driven and creative woman, who rarely sat down. When she did, she was busy knitting, sewing, writing or organizing something. She was also an amateur photographer who spent long hours in our attic developing and editing film. Her cameras went everywhere with her. Mom loved hosting elaborate parties that would fill our home with friends and co-workers. When classical or opera music played from our phonograph, I would get a glimpse of the dancing eccentric soul she longed to be.

Tanta, our maid, was a mystical grandmother who spoke to me through the wisdom in her eyes and the softness of her gnarled hands. During the day, her grip was my security blanket as she guided me down sidewalks and shopped for groceries or walked me home from the bus stop after school. She taught me to count coins in German so I could buy treats from the bakery. Other than that, she was silent. At night we shared an evening ritual that transformed her from a seventy-year-old grandma into an enchanted woman. In the soft light of a table lamp, her hands guided me to pull hair pins from the tightly wound bun at the back of her head. The last pin released a long gray braid that tumbled past her waist. She would hand me her tortoise shell comb to untangle her thin braid into silky threads until they covered her entire back. When she turned around, she would kiss me on the forehead and send me off to bed.

I loved being in her presence, for she was kind and gentle as well as strong and wise. But her silence made me wonder where she came from and what her heart was feeling. I sensed her eyes held stories she could not tell, and that I filled a lonely place in her heart.

Sisi was like a mother to me, she was younger and more playful than Gertrude. Sisi brought a sense of calm and confidence into my life. She was graceful and patient. Like Tanta, Sisi didn't speak English, yet she taught me how to cook and clean by showing me what to do. I remember sitting in silence with her for hours on end as we played games on the floor or had imaginary tea parties. Sisi loved to take Henry and me on long walks around our neighborhood. Since we lived on the corner of Fürstenbergerstrasse and Oeder Weg, we were only eight blocks from the city center and within walking distance to the Palmengarten and my father's office.

Sisi and I washing dishes.

My favorite walk was along Oeder Weg, which was lined with quaint bakeries, flower shops, butcher shops and specialty stores. I loved counting my coins in German and buying a small glass jar of yogurt, a bag of gummi bears or a special treat from the bakery. Sisi and Tanta made each shopping day feel like an adventure.

Our parents were very adventurous and loved to travel. We often drove on winding roads and hills throughout the countryside of the Main and Rhine River Valleys. Patchwork quilts defined by colorful rows of grapes, grains, vegetables and flowers floated by as I gazed out my window. I was mesmerized by the large nests built by storks perched atop chimneys in small hamlets.

Stone castles dotted the landscape; some seemed forgotten and forlorn, while others were lovingly restored with cobblestone steps and paths. We enjoyed visiting these ancient castles and discovering what was behind their stone walls or large wooden doors. We were often greeted by flowers and fountains and rows of topiary boxwoods as well as massive shade trees. One castle was filled with so much gold that it hurt my eyes. We visited little villages and ate at

Henry and I in a quaint German village.

countryside cafes. We enjoyed German sausage with brown mustard as well as wiener schnitzel and spaetzle with lemon.

In the summers we vacationed in Garmisch - Partenkirchen, a resort town in the Bavarian Alps. Massive evergreens wove these Alpine mountains together in a way that felt impenetrable. I marveled at the strength of their branches as they each held several feet of snow. They seemed like royalty, draped in white robes that glittered in the sun. In summer, the ice and snow at this higher altitude allowed me to learn how to ski and skate for the first time.

Even with all of these amazing trips, my imagination was most captivated by our home and the park next door. Our home was a seven-level villa smothered in vines, surrounded by trees and protected by a concrete wall. A green metal gate swung open to a courtyard with cobblestone paths, flower gardens and a small fruit orchard.

The Belvedere roof contained the seventh level attic as well as a sixth level that functioned as our indoor playground.

My mother's photography studio was located in the attic above. A large solid wooden door with several metal locks prevented us from walking up the stairs and into her darkroom. Her secrecy captured my curiosity. I would question my mother about what was behind the door and would beg her to let me in. One day she allowed me upstairs, but made me promise to never ask again. My excitement grew as she unlocked each lock and the door

Our home in Frankfurt.

creaked open. The penetrating odor of chemicals greeted me as we walked up a narrow dark flight of steps. When she flipped on the switch, all I saw was red. When my eyes adjusted, I saw rows of tables and trays filled with solution and photographs. Straps of wire were strung above me, holding photos and filmstrips clipped like laundry hanging out to dry. She guided me to a long bench that held a splicing machine. She told me how she could cut out sections of film and then splice them back together. She explained that she kept this space dark so her photos could develop properly, and that opening the door allowed light to come in, which is why she kept it locked. Before I could really look around, my one and only visit was over. My curiosity was satisfied, at least for now.

We walked down the stairs to our indoor playground. A full swing set and sandbox were set up on the landing in front of the door to keep us busy and out of trouble.

A series of small rooms wrapped around a large open balcony that overlooked the fifth floor below. Each room was designated as a play space. We had a room filled with toys, a kitchen room, a train room, and a doctor's office.

A grand staircase led down to an open foyer on the fifth level, where we all slept. Sisi and Heinz had their own bedroom as did Tanta. Henry and I shared a room, plus my parents had a room. There were bathrooms and guest rooms for visitors and a room we never entered.

A long L-shaped staircase led down to the fourth level, which was our primary living space. A maze of arches and vaulted ceilings made it feel like a castle. We shared the large kitchen, dining room, living room and library. The library led to a large outdoor balcony. We spent many hours sitting on the balcony, listening to the sounds of birds. A set of stairs connected the balcony to the gardens below where a swing was suspended in an old apple tree. The main entrance to the house was a two-tiered stone staircase that led past the garden level to an oversized wood door.

The garden level was technically the third level. Everything was painted white and the sun was shining through the windows that encircled it. It even had its own private side entrance. I sensed this space had been used as a makeshift hospital during the war.

The second level or basement, which was dark and musty, was used only for storage.

The first or lowest level contained a small root cellar and wine cellar as well as a bomb shelter with a shaft for ventilation.

CHAPTER 2: THE MESSAGE

Holzhausen Park was just steps from our home. It was filled with majestic old trees and cobblestone paths. Some areas felt very secret and private, while others were open and expansive. A small castle sat near the entrance of the park surrounded by a moat. Stone steps led directly into the water, where a family of white trumpeter swans lived.

Once I turned five my mother trusted me to walk to the park with my younger brother Henry. In the winter we played in the snow; during the summer I fed the swans. The trees and swans were my friends, and this park was my personal sanctuary.

Henry (right) and I (left) playing in the snow at Holzhausen Park in 1960.

It was a sunny September day in 1961, and I was almost seven years old. Henry and I were walking on one of the paths in the park, when I sensed someone near us. I stopped and looked to my left. There, inside a large old tree, I saw a beautiful woman with long dark hair and dark eyes. She was dressed in a flowing white dress. I was amazed that I could see inside the tree; as if the trunk had become translucent. She looked very serene and sweet, yet her gaze was penetrating. Her being filled the entire trunk as she was motioning for me to come near her.

I asked Henry, who was standing next to me, if he could see her but he couldn't. It scared me that I could see her so clearly, so I grabbed Henry's hand and ran to the other end of the park. Once we reached the open playground, I looked back to see if she had followed us. When I didn't see anything, I relaxed. We played in the field beyond the trees.

Later that evening, I woke up from a sound sleep and saw a cloud hovering in my bedroom. I sensed it was the lady in the tree and that I might be in trouble for seeing her or not going to her. The cloud seemed friendly and inquisitive as it began moving toward me. I hung onto the edge of my blanket as I watched it shift from white to grey, then back to white. It changed shape and swirled around the room until it was directly above me. It became motionless, time seemed to stand still. I sank into my bed and quietly wondered why she had followed me from the park into my room.

I silently asked: "What do you want of me?"

I didn't hear anything, but she shared the following words with me, as if we were in each other's minds:

You have been put on this earth
for a special purpose and
that purpose is to help people
understand each other better.

Once I received that message, she disappeared. I remember lying there in a state of total wonder. I also felt excited about helping people understand each other better.

When I woke up the next morning, as I stood at the top of the stairs stretching to wake up, I sensed someone was with me again, but when I looked around no one was there.

The stairs in front of me were very steep and I remember thinking to myself, "I wish I could fly." In that exact moment, I felt two invisible but gentle hands slip under my armpits, grasping me firmly yet tenderly.

The staircase where I felt the tree spirit carry me.

Before I realized what was happening, I was sweetly lifted from the top of the landing and was now floating down the stairs in front of me. My feet didn't touch the floor until I felt the hands slip out from under my armpits. When I turned around, no one was there.

I was amazed at how natural and effortless it all felt. I suddenly realized that the same spirit who had visited me in my sleep and who had just carried me down the staircase was the lady in the tree I had seen the day before.

Excited, I ran to my mother in the kitchen to tell her what happened. She immediately dismissed me and my "overactive imagination."

I asked her if this might be my guardian angel.

She told me, "We do have guardian angels, but we don't see them and we certainly aren't carried by them."

I thought to myself, if she isn't my guardian angel, then she must be a tree spirit. It was as if each of these three experiences reinforced each other so I would forever believe it to be true. Little did I know that my life was about to change in ways that I could never imagine.

"It is not so much for its beauty
that the forest makes a claim upon men's hearts,
as for that subtle something,
that quality of air that emanation from old trees,
that so wonderfully changes and renews a weary spirit."
- Robert Louis Stevenson -

CHAPTER 3: THE SEPARATION

Within days of meeting the Tree Spirit, which is what I came to call her, my father told us we were moving to the United States. We left our home immediately and moved into the Rhine-Main Army/Air base outside of Frankfurt.

Our move was sudden and secretive; Mom and Dad didn't tell us why we had to go. I was devastated. I didn't want to move. I had just started first grade at a new school, and I loved learning and playing with all of my new friends. I didn't want to leave my home, especially Sisi, Tanta, and Heinz. But most of all I didn't want to leave Holzhausen Park and the Tree Spirit who I felt would share more of how I was to help people understand each other better.

I sensed that my parents didn't want to move either. My father seemed deflated and empty, and my mother was angry. I was afraid to tell anyone what I was feeling. It was all very confusing as our belongings were being packed in large wooden crates and taken away.

In November 1961, we boarded the S.S. United States, a high-speed, luxury trans-Atlantic Ocean liner. When we reached the dock, I was amazed by the sheer size of this magnificent ship. Its red, black and white exterior loomed in front of me like a steel wall. Two enormous red smokestacks billowed black smoke into the gray skies.

Walking through the canvas-covered tunnel into the ship I felt that I was entering an entirely new world. The air was filled with strange sounds as bells chimed, engines roared and smokestacks blew. We walked in unison, to the clanging of luggage carts and people shuffling about searching for their cabins. Eventually we settled into ours.

The crossing took five days, the fastest recorded time in history at that time.

It was very cold and windy on the outside decks, so we mainly stayed inside. When we did go outside, we sat on wooden deck chairs as bellboys covered us in wool blankets and served cups of steaming hot beef bouillon.

The length of the ship was over 900 feet long. Henry and I explored it every day, always discovering something new. We found a movie theatre, shops and restaurants on the main deck. On one of the upper decks a dog kennel and playground area kept us busy. Deep in the belly of the ship was a swimming pool filled with salt water. Our mother supervised us as Henry and I wore musty smelling orange life vests and bobbed around in the pool like floating corks. In the evening we all dressed up for special evening meals in the main dining room.

On our fourth night, we sat at a special round table with the ship's captain. I remember him asking me what my favorite food was. I told him that I had just been introduced to honeydew melon, and how I loved that they were shaped into tiny green balls. He then ordered a large bowl of melon just for me. What a special night that was!

My parents let us stay up late to listen to a jazz band. The dining room transformed into a fancy night club with men wearing black and white tuxedos and women wearing glittering gowns. People were dancing and drinking fancy cocktails. It was all so elegant and grand.

The air was filled with anticipation as we neared our final destination, the United States of America. That night, when the chimes signaled that it was time to clear the decks, I knew this was my last night on this amazing ship, and I wondered what the next day would bring.

When I awoke, the skies were cloudy and gray. A cold drizzle obscured the view, but then I began to see a faint outline emerging through the fog and mist. We stood on the deck as the New York City skyline rose above the water. The Statue of Liberty seemed to suddenly appear as we turned into the harbor. I was mesmerized by the sheer size and strength she exuded. I felt welcomed by her to this new land as we glided toward the harbor below.

When we left the ship, we were greeted by a man standing next to a big black car. He drove us to our new home in Alexandria, VA. As we rode through the dark narrow streets of Manhattan, the skyscrapers loomed so tall that I couldn't see the sky. I had never seen skyscrapers before; I was afraid that they would fall and crush us. When we drove through a very long tunnel, I held my breath praying we would survive. When we emerged on the other side, I could see the sky again and I began to breathe. This was my first memory of actually being in the United States of America.

Our small red brick row house was very different from the grand home we had left, but I was open to a new adventure. I was introduced to American culture on a black and white television set. I remember watching commercials and *Captain Kangaroo*. I ate my first bowl of Rice Krispies, hoping to hear them snap, crackle and pop.

Every day my father left to attend meetings with government officials. Meanwhile I attended school in Alexandria, Virginia where I could see the Washington Monument from my desk. Everything about my life had changed dramatically and nothing felt certain.

In January 1962, we left our home in Washington, D.C. and moved to an apartment in Kewaunee, Wisconsin.

We were now living in an upstairs flat, three blocks from my maternal grandparents. I was excited to know my grandparents and to listen to their stories.

Grandpa Henry was a fun-loving man who loved playing a card game called Sheepshead and drank Snowshoe, a blend of peppermint schnapps and brandy. He was a carpenter and millwright who built bridges and grain elevators. My grandmother Alvinia was the opposite of my grandpa. She was stern and didn't like to talk or laugh. She did love to bake, which was something I totally appreciated. I discovered that my great grandparents had immigrated to Wisconsin in the late 1800s from Germany and Prussia. Henry and Alvinia had three children: Fritz, Gertrude and Arnold. My mother was the middle child and the only girl.

I loved living so close to my grandparents, and our home was only a few blocks from my new school. I was now in second grade, even though I hadn't finished first grade. I didn't really understand what it meant to skip ahead, but it was okay as I began to make new friends. Kewaunee was a beautiful little town. I learned to ride my bicycle in its quiet, tree-lined streets. I played with my new friends in their backyards or at the beach on Lake Michigan.

Unfortunately, there was tension between my parents. They began speaking to each other in German, which is what they did when they didn't want me to understand what they were talking about. I could tell they were upset, as their voices grew louder. It was frustrating to hear them talk in front of me, and not know what they were saying. Their tone frightened me, I had never seen them argue like this before.

Even though I could count in German, and say a few polite words, I had not been allowed to understand, speak or write German. I wanted them to be happy again, but they wouldn't let me in. My life began to be filled with secrets.

My mother began searching for her independence and had set her sights on buying Sobenia's Clover Farm Store in Algoma, Wisconsin. She wanted to operate her own business and for us to live in the upstairs apartment. My father wanted nothing to do with the store, but my mother was determined to move forward, even without his blessing.

She asked if I wanted to come with her to meet Mrs. Sobenia and see the store. Neither my father or brother joined us, but I was up for the adventure.

When we met Mrs. Sobenia, she told us it was too hard to run the store by herself, especially after her husband died. The store was originally founded in 1875, when people traveled by horse and buggy. It was a long, narrow, green two-story building. The large front door was flanked by two enormous glass windows. Inside, the high ceilings were covered in pressed tin panels. Rows of shelves filled the space below. A little bell jingled when the door moved. We were both enchanted, and Mom went forward with her plan.

Virtues Clover Farm Store - Algoma

In the summer of 1962 Mrs. Sobenia gave the keys of her store to my mom. We all moved into the apartment upstairs, but my father was not happy.

My mother renamed it Virtues Clover Farm Store. She focused her sights on selling the freshest produce, meats, dairy and cheese, like the neighborhood grocery stores in Frankfurt. This meant she was butchering her own meat, grinding coffee, slicing meat, and keeping the store filled with fresh produce and bakery. We even packed tobacco into pouches.

17

Soon after we moved in, I noticed that my parents were beginning to live completely separate lives. My mother rarely smiled and they barely spoke to each other. My father became very quiet and despondent. He was having a hard time finding a job and was struggling to redefine his life. He had taken a state civil service test, hoping for a government job. When he learned that he had earned the second highest score in Wisconsin history, offers started coming in from all over the country. Unfortunately, none of them were within driving distance of Algoma, so he turned them all down. I could sense his sadness and frustration.

My mother refused to sell the store and relocate. He refused to help her in the store, even though she asked. I wondered why my mother bought the store if my father was so against it. They were so mad at each other.

My father began taking odd jobs just to feel useful. That summer, he worked as a tax collector, traveling to various carnivals and fairs. I joined him once and saw first-hand how humiliated and unhappy he was going from trailer to trailer collecting taxes from struggling people.

Eventually, he found a job as a prison guard at the Wisconsin State Reformatory in Green Bay, a maximum-security facility. This was definitely not his dream. He worked the night shift in Green Bay and then drove bus for the Algoma Public Schools during the day. He went from no job to two jobs. I rarely saw him. He slept a few hours a day. I felt he was searching for ways to be away from my mother, but it also meant he was away from us. When he was home, they didn't talk or even look at each other.

I found myself desperately missing Sisi and Tanta. I asked my mother if she knew where they were. She told me they were in Germany and that I would never see them again. I asked her if she had their address, so I could write letters to them. She said she didn't and that I needed to let them go.

Algoma was a small lumber and fishing village located along Lake Michigan. I remembered seeing a sign that said the name "*Algoma*" was Pottawatomie for "Park of Flowers." I began to imagine that a beautiful park filled with flowers existed somewhere in this town of 2800 people. In the back of my mind, I was really hoping that the Tree Spirit had moved with me and that if I asked her to show herself, she would. I thought that if I could see her again, she might be able to help me understand what was happening to my parents and how I could help them.

I found out that the city park was only five blocks away from our home. Excitedly, I jumped on my bike to check it out. What I found was a large, flat rectangular field surrounded by chain link fencing. The park featured two dusty baseball diamonds and a grassy football field. There were worn out wooden bleachers scattered about and a little green concession stand near the entrance. On the east end was a playground with swings, slides and a merry-go-round, plus a cement wading pool in a faded shade of aqua blue.

There weren't any flowers, pathways, ponds, stone walls or swans. Only a few tall trees lined the perimeter of the fence. I stood in front of each tree but felt nothing. I sat on one of the bigger swings in the middle of the park and waited for a sign... nothing.

Then I heard the steady drone of the foghorn. It was late afternoon and the fog was beginning to roll in from Lake Michigan. I left the park and biked four blocks east to the beach. The sound of waves splashed onto the two cement piers as seagulls hovered and squawked above me. The scent of this large fresh water lake filled me with hope. I found myself surrounded by large cedars (arborvitae) blowing in the breeze as I scanned its endless blue horizon.

An old-fashioned red lighthouse punctuated the scene as it sat majestically at the end of the north pier.

The south pier was shaped like a hook, which almost touched the lighthouse across from it. A narrow channel of water flowed between them creating a barrier from the rugged waves of Lake Michigan and the peaceful waters within their grasp.

A large grove of old cedar trees lined the grassy hill that overlooked the crescent shaped beach below. I searched for a quiet place to sit and take it all in.

It was here where I finally felt my heart begin to relax. I hadn't found the Tree Spirit, but I did find a space where I felt safe enough to imagine and dream.

CHAPTER 4: THE CONFUSION

It was Labor Day weekend, the day before I was to officially start third grade in my new hometown.

We went to my Grandpa Henry's house for a family reunion. I was playing in the living room when one of my cousins showed me a photo album lying on a shelf under the TV. There were pictures of my mother's family, and it was fun to see their faces and learn their names. I was beginning to realize how wonderful it was to live so close to my cousins here in America and how we were all one big family.

As I flipped through the pages, I came to a picture of myself as a baby. It had typing all over it and looked more like a postcard than a photo. As I read it, I was shocked!

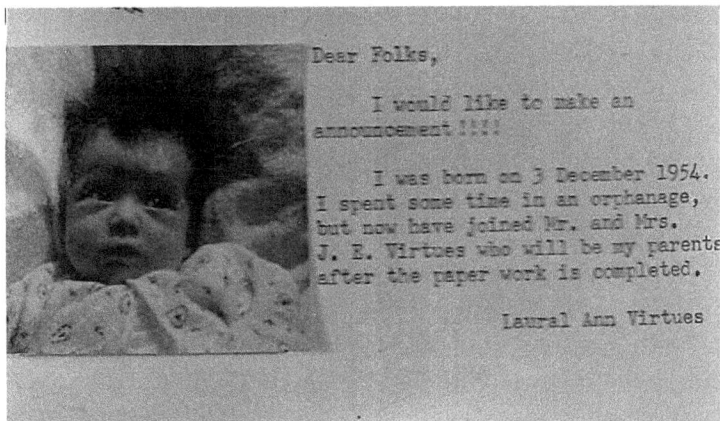

Dear Folks, I would like to make an announcement!!!!
I was born on 3 December 1954. I spent some time in an
orphanage, but now have joined Mr. and Mrs. J. E. Virtues who
will be my parents after the paperwork is completed.

What was this? Reading the word "orphanage" made my mind race in total disbelief. This isn't my family? This isn't my mother and father? I ran into the kitchen where my mother and grandmother were sitting.

Holding the photo album in my arms I cried, "Mom! Mom, am I adopted? What does this mean?"

My mom replied very matter-of-factly, "Yes, you were, but I don't want to talk about it."

My mother had become stronger and more willful. Now when she said no, it meant no! I pulled deep inside myself; I was totally confused and completely devastated. Meanwhile, my grandmother Alvina just shook her head with disgust. I stood there clutching the photo album to my chest as my grandmother told the story of how she had called my mother in Frankfurt after receiving the card I just found.

She recounted her words, "Gertrude, out of all the babies you could have adopted, why did you pick such a homely one?" My mother said nothing, as I think she was in as much shock as I was. I needed love and affection so desperately in that very moment, but neither of them seemed willing or able to give it to me. I couldn't understand how any of this could be happening. My mind was desperately trying to comprehend what I had just learned, and the silence coming from my mother was deafening.

My father had been outside drinking beer with my grandpa. When he came in and realized what had happened, he motioned for us all to get in the car immediately. My father didn't say a word, but I could tell he was furious.

The drive back to Algoma was surreal as tension filled the car. I gazed out the window toward Lake Michigan and dreamed of my home in Germany beyond its shores. I cried in silence as tears streamed down my cheeks. I knew in that moment that I was very, very far from my home.

From that day on, my entire life turned upside down in a way that I can't describe. I felt empty inside; the betrayal in my heart was so deep and heavy that I could barely breathe. How could everything I know be a lie?

Feelings of being abducted began to overwhelm me, as I realized that these were not my real parents, my real grandparents, or my real home. I wondered who my actual parents were and how this had happened to me.

I was missing my life in Germany so desperately that I began begging the Tree Spirit to find me and help me understand what had happened. I needed someone to tell me that everything was going to be all right, but no one did.

I walked to school the very next morning in a daze. It was September 1962, and I was now beginning third grade. This was my fifth school in nine months. Everything had changed in my life. I was wishing that Sisi or Tanta were there to hold my hand like they had so many times before. I was seven years old and my entire world had collapsed.

As I settled into my desk, our teacher asked us to go around the room and introduce ourselves by explaining who we were and where we were born. My heart began to race. When it was my turn to talk, the only thing I could say was, "I'm not sure I was even born because I'm adopted. What I do know is that I come from Frankfurt, Germany, but for all I know I could have been hatched!"

The whole class started laughing at me. I don't remember if our teacher said anything or not. All I know is that I felt very alone and that I didn't want to be there.

Some of my classmates made fun of me and bullied me because I was different. To escape, I hid behind bushes and trees. They began to call me "Hitler" or "Hitler's daughter," saying that he was my father and that he was killed in Germany, which is why I was an orphan. I had never heard of Hitler before, so I began wondering if this was true.

There was a great deal of hatred toward Germany, which was hard for me to understand. I loved Germany and was missing everything about it.

By the end of that first week of school, everyone was on edge. To soften the mood my father drove us to Green Bay to visit my other grandparents, John and Laura Virtues.

These grandparents lived in a simple two-story white house in the Broadway District of Green Bay. Their neighborhood was bordered by factories, including a pickle company. The intoxicating smell of vinegar hung in the air.

My father John was their only child and we were their only grandchildren. It was easy to feel loved by them. My grandfather, John Virtues Sr., born in 1887, was a tall, handsome man who loved reading, listening to music and playing the fiddle. He smoked a brown wooden pipe that made the house smell exotic and old. I would sit with him on the couch and listen to Milwaukee Braves baseball or Green Bay Packers football on his stand-up radio. He always wore a dress shirt with a vest or button-down sweater. He was an entrepreneurial man who had owned a lumber mill in Greenleaf and later a hardware store on Broadway Street.

My grandfather John was the oldest of eleven children. His father, also named John Virtues, came to the United States in 1864 to start a new life. He was only eleven years old. His parents had died of diphtheria in Prussia, leaving him and his half-sister to fend for themselves. Together they boarded a steamship out of Hamburg, Germany. When my great-grandfather arrived in America, he changed his surname from Furstenau to "Virtues" because that's what he felt America stood for. Eventually he came to Wisconsin and homesteaded a parcel of land north of Green Bay. It was amazing to me how his story sounded somewhat like mine; I wanted to know as much as I could about my great-grandfather and his immigration story.

24

My grandfather was a wonderful storyteller and he loved sharing his family history with me. During one of our visits, he told me the story of how my great-grandfather obtained 26 signatures from nearby farmers to request the authorization of a school district in Little Suamico, Wisconsin. He wanted his children to be educated, so he created the area's first one-room schoolhouse in 1894. My grandfather would have turned eight that year, so he was one of its first students. He took me up to the attic, which smelled of dry wood and musty paper, to show me photos of the schoolhouse and the farmhouse he grew up in. His attic was a treasure chest of antiques and curiosities. I loved it!

My grandmother, Laura Virtues, was born in 1883 to a large farming family with Danish roots. Whenever we came to visit, she wore an embroidered cotton apron over a calico dress. She always baked a fresh batch of sugar cookies just for Henry and me, which meant there would be flour dust and cookie sheets scattered across the kitchen counter. Henry and I played under their large, round oak dining room table waiting for the cookies to cool.

My grandmother Virtues had been a schoolteacher her entire life, teaching in one-room schoolhouses throughout northeastern Wisconsin and upper Michigan. In 1908, she was the teacher for the school my great grandfather started. It was here, as the teacher of my grandfather's younger siblings, that my grandparents met. Laura was five years older than John. They were married in 1915, when she was 32 and he was 28. My father was born one year later in 1916. They named him John as well.

Within months of falling in love with my grandpa and grandma Virtues, I discovered that my grandmother was dying of ovarian cancer. The last time we went to visit her there were no sugar cookies. The house felt heavy and sad. My grandpa Virtues asked me if I wanted to see Grandma.

I quietly walked into her bedroom; the shades were pulled and the air was still as I sat at her bedside. She rolled over and looked at me with love and resolve.

She told me that my mother had named me Laural, after her and my grandmother, Alvinia. I was her only granddaughter; she wanted me to know that I was loved and cherished. Then she reached into her nightstand and handed me her precious gold pocket watch. It had a pair of birds, plus her initials, engraved upon it. They were the same as mine, LAV. She tenderly pressed the watch into my hands and fell asleep. She passed away ten days later, just before my eighth birthday.

The grandmother who loved me was now gone. The longing in my heart to feel loved and safe felt more and more elusive. The memories of feeling special and cared for seemed so long ago and out of reach. I felt that any remnant of my fairytale life was now officially over.

I tried to find peace in my new life by walking to Lake Michigan and strolling along the docks lined with old fish shanties, or sitting under the cedars along the sandy beach. My other sacred place was the Ahnapee River, which was two blocks away. Both instilled a sense of adventure.

I entered fourth grade that fall hoping it would be better. But I soon discovered that I was still an outsider. One day, during recess, we were racing and I won the race. Instead of allowing me to feel good about winning, the other kids jumped on me and started kicking me. I curled into a ball like an armadillo. When the bell rang and recess was over, they all ran back into school, leaving me on the ground by myself. I looked up and realized I was under a cluster of cedar trees in the corner of the playground. It was odd, but I sensed they witnessed my humiliation without judgment.

In that moment I felt an inner knowing that they were letting me know that they understood the truth of what was happening to me and that they loved me unconditionally.

A few weeks later, on November 22, 1963 I heard the announcement over the school's PA system that President Kennedy had been assassinated. I was hiding in the girl's bathroom, something I often did during recess. I didn't feel safe in the United States and this made it worse. Nothing made sense. Why in the world did we come here?

I continued trying to connect with the Tree Spirit from Holzhausen Park. I sat on the banks of Lake Michigan under the cedar trees and looked east toward Germany. I was hoping that the water and air could carry my message to her as they flowed from Algoma all the way across the Atlantic Ocean and beyond. I sensed that she could find me, as long as I kept letting her know where I was.

I also sat inside clusters of cedars as a safe place to hide between the school and our house. I regularly walked a certain path so I could feel them along the way. These trees became my first real American friends. I also felt safe in our yard, which was completely surrounded by a thick wall of cedars. Many years later I learned that these trees were actually arborvitaes, which in Latin means "Tree of Life."

It was clear to my mother that neither Henry or I were adjusting to public school in Algoma. I was now graduating from fourth grade, but Henry was being held back in first grade. Her solution was to place us into the Door-Kewaunee Normal School so we could "settle down." This wasn't a "normal school," it was a teacher's college with only a handful of students, and it was located right next to the public school.

I was the only student in fifth grade. They often placed me in a little room by myself with no windows and gave me tests or books to read. Different teachers would come in and talk with me. My mind drifted as I became more withdrawn and isolated.

One night, my parents left Henry and me home alone, so they could attend my mother's high school reunion in Kewaunee. Henry went to bed, while I sat up and watched television. As I searched the three channels available to us, I came upon a black and white documentary about Hitler and the Holocaust. Since I wanted to learn who Hitler was and why my classmates hated him and Germany, I decided to watch it. I was curious at first, but soon I was horrified, yet I couldn't stop watching. I was frozen with terror and propelled by my insatiable curiosity. I sensed this was my only chance to learn the truth about Hitler, where I was born and the secrets that surrounded me. The scenes were very graphic and disturbing. I had no idea that Germany had started a war, or that innocent people had been captured, tortured and killed in such mass numbers. When I looked at the faces of the children, mothers, fathers, grandparents, etc... I saw myself in them. I didn't look anything like Hitler. I felt a deep sense of guilt for the people who had been destroyed by the very man I feared could be my father. The cameras focused on rows and rows of people dead or dying, lying in piles on dirt roads in camps surrounded by wire. The Germany I knew that was filled with wonder was now the home to one of the most horrific events on Earth.

I began to understand why no one liked me - it was because I was German. I could feel a part of me slip away as my innocence disappeared into the darkness of war.

I continued to watch even though I was getting physically ill. My stomach was in knots, but I had to know what had happened to Hitler.

I had to know if he had lived through the war and if he could actually be my father. Scene after scene of horror beyond measure made me so sick that eventually I ran to the bathroom and vomited. But even that didn't stop me, I returned more determined to find out the truth.

At the end of the program, I was relieved to know that Hitler had died in 1945, nine years before I was born. My fear of this monster being my father was gone, but the reality of what I had just witnessed sank in. I was so distraught that I called the place where my mother and father were and pleaded for them to come home.

By the time my parents got home I was completely exhausted and terrified. My father didn't say anything, my mother was mad. Neither wanted to talk about what I had just seen. I really wished they would have helped me understand how this had happened and if it had anything to do with why we left Germany or why I was adopted.

From that point on I was prohibited from watching TV without her consent. I understood why she was upset, but I knew in my heart that I needed to see this to find some of the answers to the questions I had, especially since no one wanted to talk about the Holocaust or World War II.

My life continued to be a complete and total mystery. How was I ever going to help people understand each other better if I couldn't understand myself? I wondered why the Tree Spirit told me I had a special purpose and then left me to figure this all out alone.

My mother was now realizing that the Door-Kewaunee Normal School wasn't working for us either, so she sent us back to public school. I entered sixth grade with a deep sense of shame and sadness. I didn't feel the pride and joy of being German like I had before. I didn't see myself as an American either. Plus, the year at the Normal School had made me more withdrawn.

My grades suffered because I wasn't motivated to learn anymore. I hadn't made any friends, and I was still being beaten or bullied for being "weird." I would come home crying after school and go straight to my room.

One day my mother saw how sad I was and asked, "What did you get into now?"

When I told her what was happening, she said, "You must be doing something wrong."

I tried to understand what I was doing wrong, but it didn't make any sense to me. I had no one to talk to, not even my brother Henry. He was very different than I, more outgoing and mischievous.

John, Gertrude, Henry and I in Algoma – 1964.

I started having night terrors that made me throw up in the middle of the night. My mother would wake up to check on me.

She would say, "Don't worry, it's only the meanness coming out."

It was an odd statement that made me fear that something mean was actually within me. I started wondering what sort of "meanness" I had. This caused me to begin feeling guilty for things I didn't do or understand.

Then one day our sixth-grade teacher told us we were going to read *The Diary of Anne Frank* and do a play. She shared with the class that since I was from Germany I would be cast as Anne Frank. I was shocked, but I knew in my heart that she was trying to help me, and I appreciated her for it.

She was in her late sixties and she reminded me of Tanta. I could sense the wisdom and empathy in her eyes.

As she handed me the book, I saw Anne's face on the cover. It was like looking into a mirror. Her story inspired me to start journaling my own thoughts as a way to express and release my feelings. My mother could see that I was becoming interested in books again, so she gave me a set of illustrated books of the Old and New Testament. I was fascinated by the stories and the images as I read them over and over again. I felt a connection with Jesus. His teachings inspired me to see that I needed to learn from the pain and see the lessons it holds. By doing this I could begin to understand myself and others.

I don't have any memories of going to church in Germany, but here it became clear that my parents were both devout Christians. My father was Catholic and my mother was Lutheran, which was somewhat scandalous at the time. They were married in a court house without their parents in attendance. My mother also volunteered as a Sunday school teacher at her Missouri Synod Lutheran Church.

During the summer of 1966, my mother, who was the President of the VFW Auxiliary in Algoma, told me that I was going to be the Poppy Queen!

Me as the Poppy Queen - 1966

The Memorial Day parade was the VFW's biggest event of the year, and she was in charge of making the VFW floats. I was excited about being the Poppy Queen until I learned that she wanted to make me look like an enormous poppy! Every other Poppy Queen before me wore beautiful dresses. I tried to talk her out of it, but it was no use.

31

When the big day came, there I was with a large piece of red vinyl around my neck, a ball of green mesh bunched on top of my head, and a solid green jumper covering me from head to toe. I sat on top of a cherry red, 1966 Chevy convertible waving my "leaves" to everyone in town. To my horror the local paper had a photo of me in all my glory on the front page of the paper! The humiliation of riding around the streets of Algoma looking like a poppy flower convinced me that I had nothing more to lose.

I entered junior high with a defiant sense of inner strength. The teachings of Jesus and his philosophy of "turn the other cheek" vs. "an eye for an eye" inspired me to practice peace yet stand up for what I believed. I was done hiding, which meant that I asked more questions and began to challenge my teachers. I was curious about life, but some of my teachers didn't appreciate it.

My science teacher would get irritated whenever I started a sentence with "I think." He would say, "Virtues, don't think. It's dangerous." Everyone would laugh.

One day he showed a filmstrip about proper classroom behavior. During the film, there was a clip of someone who disrupted the class by asking annoying questions. Everyone started laughing and he got very mad. As he tried to settle the class down, he told us that we all had to write a 1000-word essay about proper classroom behavior.

When the class began to moan and complain, he added, "Well, we all know why you reacted the way you did, and we all know who was responsible!"

At that instant, everyone turned around, stared at me, and glared. My heart sank with embarrassment.

He then told the class, "If you want to show that person how you feel, go right ahead! Just don't do it in the school building or during class time."

I couldn't believe what I was hearing!

When recess came, I went to my safe haven in the bathroom and hid for a while to gain my composure and decide what to do. This was getting really old, and I was sick of hiding and being afraid. I was hoping that no one would really want to hurt me, so I left the safety of the school's bathroom and headed out the doors to the playground area.

I felt like Daniel walking into the Colosseum. It was the middle of winter, and the snowplows had created a huge semicircle of tall snow piles. When I saw that none of my classmates were on the playground, I curiously walked forward. When I neared the snow piles my classmates popped up from the mounds and descended upon me. All I remember is being kicked and called names. I curled into my familiar ball, hoping to shield myself from getting kicked in the face. As soon as the bell rang, they ran back into school.

As I pulled myself together, I could see that I was bleeding and that my clothes were torn. I didn't want to go back into school looking like this so I decided to walk home.

On the way home I wondered what I was supposed to learn from this. Should I not be brave? Should I not ask questions? Should I remain silent?

I opened the back door and tried to walk silently up the stairs hoping she wouldn't hear me. But she did. and yelled from the front of the store, "Why are you home so early?" I froze at the bottom of the stairs as she approached. When she saw me, she gasped and went silent.

For the first time, she wasn't angry at me. Instead, she asked, "What happened to you?"

My mother Gertrude in her store.

33

After I told her she immediately went to the school to confront my teacher. She even went to the next school board meeting and filed an official complaint. From that point on, my mother became more involved in what was happening to me at home and at school. Her take-charge attitude inspired me, as I realized I also needed to take charge of my life. She would tell me, "If you want something done you have to do it yourself." Surprisingly Mom hired someone to help with the store so she could spend time more with us and her other responsibilities with the VFW, church and school board.

Since my mother played the organ at her church, she encouraged me to learn how to play as well. I took piano lessons from our neighbor and signed up to join the junior high school band. Since my instrument was the cornet, I immediately learned how to play taps so I could join Mom and the VFW honor guard on Memorial Day. For the next five years, beginning in 1967, I played taps after the gun salute at each cemetery in our area. It was a solemn and humbling experience to see how many graves were marked with American flags. Most were from WWI, WWII and the Korean War, but this year we had also lost our first soldier from the Vietnam War. He was 19 and a Marine Corps rifleman who had attained the rank of corporal. I had seen him at school and at church, so it really hit home. In total, our small town buried three young men who lost their lives in Vietnam. It put my problems into perspective.

By the summer of 1968 riots were happening in cities and towns across U.S., Martin Luther King Jr. and Robert F. Kennedy had both been assassinated. It was a time of great upheaval, as young men were being drafted against their will, some enlisted while others became draft dodgers.

My transistor radio was my lifeline to the outside world. It sat on the windowsill in my bedroom, positioned just right so I could listen to WLS out of Chicago. I consumed music as if it were air. The Byrds, Buffalo Springfield, the Doors, Jimi Hendrix and the Beatles spoke to my soul. Their songs made me feel less lonely and hopeful that together we could make the world a better place.

That fall I went back to school with a renewed sense of hope, but my freshman year in high school brought a whole new set of unexpected challenges. The biggest was girl's gym class. We now had to take group showers, which meant my classmates would see me naked. The first time I walked into the shower I was taunted for being a "child" because I was 13 and undeveloped. During gym class they would snap open my gym suit to expose the fact that I was still wearing a t-shirt. I felt so inadequate and humiliated.

My mother wasn't a very feminine woman and she refused to buy me a bra because she felt I didn't need one. She didn't understand the peer pressure I was under.

One day after I showered, a group of girls pushed me naked into my gym locker and locked the door. They poured hot water through the top of the locker. I could hear them laughing as the water dripped on my shivering body. I held myself and cried. I was stuck in that locker for over an hour before the male janitor heard me and let me out.

A few weeks later, this same group of girls grabbed me naked from the shower room and forced me into the outside window wells. They locked the window behind me. I had no choice but to walk along an underground set of window wells until I found an open window. I crawled into the boiler room, my arms crossed over my body, trying to figure out a way back. I hid in a corner, behind the roaring furnace until everyone was gone, and then ran to my locker.

I was so freaked out I didn't tell anyone, especially my mother. This felt very different than the bullying I had received in grade school or junior high. I didn't want to bring attention to myself and I came to dread gym class. I asked my mother, once again, to please buy me a bra. Instead, she brought me to the doctor's office to find out what was "wrong with me." I remember sitting on the exam table as she told the doctor how concerned she was that I wasn't "developing." The doctor calmly explained to her that I was a "late bloomer." He pointed out that I was also a year younger than the other girls in my grade.

When we got in the car, my mother admitted to me that she shouldn't have allowed me to jump ahead in school because I wasn't mature enough to handle it, but that now it was too late to change. I sat there silently wondering if life would be any different if I were still in eighth grade.

A few days later, a mysterious envelope appeared on my lunch tray in the cafeteria at school. I opened it and soon realized that it wasn't friendly. Whoever wrote it was making fun of me, and that I used big words to make myself sound important. As I continued reading, I noticed that most of the words came straight out of a Thesaurus. The intention was to make fun of me because of my vocabulary and to convince me that I was dumb and not liked by anyone. From that point on I became more aware of my words and began to consciously "dumb myself down" as another way to fit in.

Before Easter, I gave each of the girls sitting at my lunch table a chocolate bunny as a gift. One of them asked me to get her a glass of chocolate milk, so I did. When I returned, the girls were gone and my tray was filled with crushed wet bunnies. They left a note saying they had thrown them in the toilet and didn't want them.

I felt everyone in the cafeteria was in on it except me.

Horrified, I hid under a stairwell. Eventually my gym teacher came looking for me. I sensed she knew what was happening and was determined to find me.

It was around this time that I started having recurring dreams. One was of a large brown bear chasing me up a tree but never catching me. The second was of me flying through tree branches and over the tops of forests. Each dream gave me the chance to fly higher. The third dream was the most involved. I would be in a car traveling really fast up and down large hills. The car would go faster and faster until it flew off the road and landed on a small bridge leading to a forested island. An elephant at the entrance of the island would raise his trunk to greet me. On the island, I lived in a small log cabin in the woods with bears, wolves and deer outside. In every dream, I would explore another part of the woods, but eventually I would run back to the cabin because the bears or wolves would get too close. The more I trusted them, the more I could explore the woods.

These dreams encouraged me to explore the woods along the Ahnapee River near our home. I created a raft with logs from the local lumberyard and a rope I purchased from the hardware store with my allowance. I used a long branch as a pole to push the raft down the river. No one else was ever around, so it was secluded and safe. I loved going into the heart of the river where the tops of the cedars touched to create a tunnel. I would gaze into the crystal-clear water and admire all the colorful stones. Minnows, polliwogs and the occasional trout would swim by.

This is where I went to recharge my spirit. Here I could live in peace and leave everything else behind.

I dreamed of a world that loved me.

"I think of the trees and how simply they let go."
- May Sarton -

CHAPTER 5: LETTING GO

By the summer of 1969, I had decided to let go of being from Germany, or having a special purpose told to me by the Tree Spirit in Holzhausen Park. I so desperately wanted to feel like a normal American teenager. I was tired of hearing the same answers to my questions about what happened to Sisi, Heinz and Tanta and receiving, "I don't know" or "I don't want to talk about it." I did continue asking very direct questions about my adoption and if either of my parents knew anything about my biological parents. I would ask at the dinner table, which was the only time we were all together. My father would go completely silent and my mother would hold her breath in such a way that I felt both fear and rage pouring out of her. The silence and tension were palpable as I felt my heart beat. Finally, my mother would break the silence by declaring once again, "This is none of your business and you need to stop asking us these questions!"

We had a small television set that sat at the end of our kitchen table. Instead of talking to each other we all watched the news during dinner, which was not good for my digestive system.

Clearly my mother and father wanted me to stop thinking of Germany and everything it represented. Their solution was to take a vacation out West. We hopped into our camel-colored 1967 Chevy station wagon towing a turquoise blue pop-up camper. We camped in the Black Hills, visited Mount Rushmore and the Corn Palace. We camped at Yellowstone National Park and Jackson Hole.

39

My parents' strategy seemed to work. We were finally having fun being together other again. I actually saw them laugh and be playful with us and each other ...just like they used to be when we lived in Germany.

That summer I also made my first American friend, Pam. Her father was a local doctor, and her mother was a free spirit. She was the type of friend I wanted and needed: adventurous, inquisitive, and intelligent. We'd have sleepovers and hold séances. We often spent our time together dreaming and talking about anything and everything that interested us. Pam even invited me to her cottage in Door County with her parents on July 20, 1969. I was now fourteen years old. It was a magical night, as we laid on our stomachs on the top bunk watching TV, while Neil Armstrong walked on the moon. I will never forget the words "The Eagle has landed" and "One small step for man, one giant leap for mankind." Pam and I ran immediately outside to look at the moon. It was a beautiful, clear night, and we could see it perfectly. We tried to see the astronauts walking on the moon's surface. Of course, we couldn't, but just trying made my heart soar. I knew then that anything was possible. I was grateful to be alive, for there was so much happening in our world.

This was the summer of Woodstock and the growing counter culture that surrounded it. I was too young to go, but I consumed everything I could in order to live vicariously through those that went. I taped posters on my bedroom walls, burned incense, hung beads and listened to music.

The Beatles had just released Abbey Road, which inspired me to dream outside of myself. I felt especially connected to John Lennon and most of the bands from the British invasion like the Animals, Kinks, Donovan etc.

When I walked the foggy streets of Algoma, especially at dusk, I imagined that I was in London. I held a clear bubble umbrella over my head, wore Slicker lipstick on my lips and fishnet stockings on my legs. I wrote poetry and drew fashion designs. I started to buy funky vintage clothes from St. Vincent de Paul. My personal sense of style began to emerge. I enjoyed being "different" in an eccentric artsy hippie sort of way.

That fall, I began sophomore year in Algoma's new high school. Up until that point, the old Algoma Public School contained kindergarten through twelfth grade in one building. This new high school offered us all a fresh start.

Pam had moved away before school started, but with her friendship I had become much more confident in myself. I got involved in almost every activity the school offered. I played trumpet in our band, joined forensics and a one-act play, ski club, French club and girls' track. I even wrote the horoscope section for our high-school newspaper. I didn't have a lot of friends but I also didn't have enemies, which felt pretty good to me.

Toward the end of my junior year, my mother allowed me to participate in an exchange program with Riverside High School. Riverside was a large inner-city school in Milwaukee; we in turn were a small rural school in Algoma. My exchange student was David, who spent a week at our house. He was handsome and sensitive, with dark curly hair. We stayed up late every night to talk about the world, religion, politics, music and more. It was so wonderful to talk with someone who openly shared his thoughts about his Jewish faith and political beliefs. Our conversations gave me even more confidence in myself and my intellect.

41

He validated me in many ways, which was a tremendous gift. After David's visit, I felt unlocked. The eccentric side of me – the artist – was ready to move on, and I was looking forward to college. We wrote letters to each other for the next four years.

He moved to Israel as part of the Zionist movement. David learned Hebrew and worked as a farmer on a kibbutz. I never revealed to him my thoughts and fears surrounding the Holocaust, nor my encounter with a tree spirit in Germany. I was afraid he wouldn't believe me. I hardly believed it myself anymore.

I graduated from Algoma High School in 1972 and spent the summer preparing to begin a whole new life as a college student in the fall. I entered the University of Wisconsin-Eau Claire in September with a desire to earn a Bachelor of Fine Arts degree. I was assigned to Sutherland Hall, a dorm for girls. I was looking forward to starting over, meeting new people and making friends.

Soon after I arrived, I received a call from Steve who was just beginning his junior year at Eau Claire. We knew each other because we were both from Algoma and our parents were longtime friends through the VFW. He invited me to come over to meet his roommates.

This is where I met Wendy, his roommate Paul's girlfriend. As it turned out, Wendy and I were both freshmen living in the same dorm. We became immediate friends. She was silly, sweet and smart. Five weeks into the school year, Wendy told me she had to go home to Brodhead, Wisconsin, for the weekend to get fitted for a friend's wedding. We planned to get together that Sunday night when she got back.

Sunday night came, and I couldn't find her. Finally, I called her boyfriend's house to see if she was there. Steve answered the phone.

I asked, "Is Wendy there?"

He very matter-of-factly said, "No, she's dead."

I told him to stop joking; that this wasn't funny. Then he went on to explain that this wasn't a joke – that she had been killed in a car accident. I froze. I couldn't talk. Steve asked me if I was okay, I said "no" and hung up.

I sat there thinking this had to be a really bad dream; how could this be real? How could my first friend at college be dead? She was only 18 and full of life!

By Tuesday morning, I found myself riding in the car with Paul, Wendy's high-school sweetheart, for the three-hour drive down to Brodhead. We both sat silently in the back seat and held hands to comfort one another.

When we arrived, I remember walking into the back of this little church and he was gripping my hand so tight that it went numb. We just stood in the back; he didn't want to go in any farther. His pain was so deep that I totally forgot mine. All I wanted to do was help him get through this however I could. After the service, he began sobbing uncontrollably. When his family and friends saw him, they quickly gathered around him and took him away.

I wasn't sure what to do. I didn't know anyone at the church, and I didn't have a car. I saw Wendy's roommate, Debbie, looking for someone to go home with her. I asked her if she would like me to come, and she said "yes."

We went to her parents' home in Wauwatosa, Wisconsin, and instantly bonded. Debbie was silly, witty and fun to be with. She was very loving and hugged everyone – something I had never done before. After weeks of talking to the head resident at our dorm, I was allowed to become Debbie's roommate. In a strange and beautiful way, Wendy had guided me to the person who would become my best friend for the rest of my life. I moved in with Debbie in January 1973.

Within days of moving in an odd thing happened. We were both sleeping and the phone began to ring above my head in a very weird way. It woke me up and I started to scream, "Don't pick it up! It's a death ring!"

Debbie thought I was nuts and told me to answer the phone, which was above my head. When I did, the voice on the other end said faintly, "Goodbye, Laural," and hung up.

I knew instinctively that it was my Grandpa Virtues. I felt something was wrong and started crying hysterically.

Debbie told me to call my mother, but I told her I couldn't; I was afraid that my mom would get mad at me because it was so late. My mother called me very early the next morning to tell me that Grandpa had died the night of 1/20/1973 at 11:00 p.m. I received the call at 2:00 a.m. on 1/21/1973. When I asked Mom about the time discrepancy, she thought I was being dramatic and totally dismissed me.

As I rode the Greyhound bus to Algoma for my grandfather's funeral, I had a vision about one of our neighbors. I saw a front-page story in the *Algoma Record Herald* that featured the life of Mr. Nell who lived just down the street from us. The story I saw was a tribute of his life because he had just died. When I got off the bus, I asked my mother if she had seen the article. My mother looked at me like I was crazy. With disgust in her voice, she told me, "Mr. Nell didn't die, you better stop this foolishness right now!" She was right; that very afternoon I saw Mr. Nell with my own eyes walk by our house. I thought maybe I was going crazy or my imagination was in overdrive.

A week after returning to Eau Claire, the Algoma Record Herald arrived in the mail and there was the story I had visualized! Mr. Nell died the day after I saw him, and the paper had done a tribute exactly as I had seen it! When I called Mom, she agreed it was odd and began to search the telephone records on the night my grandfather died.

When she didn't find any record of a long-distance call to me, I could sense my mother beginning to wonder if some of what I was telling her was real. These unexplainable events seemed to come and go at random, but when I talked to my mother about it, she said it was the work of the devil. I was so hurt, confused and frustrated by her response, because I didn't see this as evil.

I began seeking a spiritual community that would understand what I was feeling without being judged.

Debbie showed me a brochure for the Campus Crusades for Christ. They were having a gathering on campus that weekend. We decided to attend. At first, their message was all about love and peace, but then it shifted to "those who don't accept Jesus as their Lord and Savior would go to hell and not be saved." We both left and never looked back. To me this was another example of how Christianity had disconnected itself from the compassionate teachings of Jesus that I felt in my heart. It seemed no one wanted to talk about spiritual experiences, non-judgment or loving others unconditionally. Instead, it seemed to be based on fear and a very narrow set of rules and dogma.

Losing Wendy and my grandfather was a lot for me to deal with. They were both people I loved, and their deaths affected me on multiple levels. Wendy's death was so sudden and senseless. My grandfather was much older and had lived a long life. I needed some quiet time away from the dorms so I could journal my feelings without being distracted. I decided to go for a drive and sleep in my car. It turned out to be a very cold February night so I checked into the Antler's Motel outside of Eau Claire. A few weeks later, my mother called, yelling at me because she received the cancelled check for the Antler's Motel. She accused me of "shacking up with some guy."

I was horrified by her accusation, especially since I had never been intimately involved with anyone. I tried to explain that I just needed to get away from the dorms to be by myself so I could reflect and think about life. She begrudgingly accepted my explanation, but said that Debbie was a bad influence.

Through all of this, I felt fortunate to have Debbie as my friend. But my mother didn't approve of her at all. Debbie could hear my mother's rage over the phone. She encouraged me to stand up to her, but I struggled to do that.

I was also struggling with my freshman English comp class. When I handed in my very first term paper, the professor asked if I had taken any English courses in high school. When she noticed that I was an art major, she challenged me to summarize the next reading assignment into a single drawing versus a term paper. She also wanted me to begin regular tutoring sessions with an English major and to go to the guidance department to be tested for a learning disability. I agreed.

A week later I took several tests along with an MMPI (Minnesota Multiphasic Personality Inventory). When they shared the results, they said I was very intelligent, but I had a very complex and circular reasoning system. Based on that, they wrote a note that made me exempt from multiple choice or true/false tests. I now had the option to request essay tests whenever I wanted. Wow! I knew this would make my life much easier, as I truly struggled with multiple-choice tests but had never understood why. They explained that I was also slightly dyslexic. I had a hard time distinguishing my right hand from my left because it required linear thinking that didn't make sense to me.

A graduate psychology student overheard that I was an art major and asked if I would be interested in doing a series of drawings for an assignment. He was creating a new psychological test and would pay me ten dollars per illustration. I agreed and drew twenty illustrations that included puddles, trees, caves, baseball bats, gloves etc. I sensed they were subtle images that represented male or female. When I turned them in, he asked me if I knew what they were for. I told him that I thought he was testing people to see if they unconsciously related to feminine or masculine imagery. He was pleased that I "got it." He told me about the groundbreaking work of Carl Jung and how the collective unconscious impacts our conscious mind. I was intrigued that art and psychology could work together on this level.

I went home that summer to work as an assistant art teacher for the summer elementary school art program. I enjoyed working with children and seeing them create.

In late July I was feeling sick and passed out during one of my classes. I walked over to the doctor's office. He diagnosed me with rheumatic heart disease, anemia and bronchial pneumonia! He wanted to put me in the hospital for observation, but my mother wouldn't have it.

I was exhausted, but determined to go back to Eau Claire and begin my sophomore year. I quietly packed up my stuff and drove straight to the dorms where Debbie was waiting for me. When I told her how depleted I felt, she said we needed to see Leo Buscaglia, "The Love Doctor." He had written several best-selling books on love and was giving a lecture in Eau Claire, so we went. His speech was all about how love heals all wounds…and that hugs are the best medicine. After hearing him speak, I was inspired to call my mother and tell her that I loved her. She got upset and told me to stop playing games and just say what I wanted.

I said, "I simply want you to know that I love you."

She said I didn't need to say that, and hung up.

Fortunately, my relationship with my father was sweeter, but we didn't see each other often. He always called me "peaches," and would flash this beautiful, warm smile that had "I love you" written all over his face. His mannerisms reminded me of a mix of John Wayne, Johnny Cash, and Don Ho.

My father was applying to be a teacher within the Wisconsin correctional system. I approached my criminal justice professor and told him about my father and the work he did. My professor was thrilled at the idea of having him as a guest speaker. When I talked to my father about it, he was excited and I could feel a spark ignite within him.

I also asked to see his resume so I could properly introduce him to the class, and it arrived a few days later. It was fascinating to read that in 1935 he volunteered for the Coast Guard and worked as a motorcycle officer for the Brown County Sheriff's Department. In 1943 he was drafted into the Army Air Force. He served as a B-29 crew chief at Alamogordo Air Base, in New Mexico. He was present for the Trinity nuclear test in July 1945. He returned to Green Bay as a detective for the Sheriff's Department. In 1947 he traveled to Maryland for counter intelligence training. He served as a special agent for the CIC (Counter Intelligence Corps), stationed in Frankfurt, Germany. In 1953 the CIC became the CIA, and my father was appointed as the Chief of an investigation and surveillance unit in Frankfurt until December 1961. From that point on, he worked as a correctional officer at the Brown County Reformatory, a maximum-security prison in Green Bay, Wisconsin.

I was so proud of him as he stood in front of the class. He was composed and solid. The teacher later told me how impressive he was as a man and as a speaker.

After class, my father invited Debbie and me out for lunch before he drove back to Algoma. I had so many questions, but it didn't seem like the right time or place to ask him about his time in the military or CIA. He was so happy to have the chance to speak to a college class.

A few weeks later, I drove home for a visit. I wanted to talk to my parents and ask them how my father's career had impacted their lives. I was ten miles from home when a pick-up truck started flashing its headlights at me. I soon realized it was my father, so I pulled over. When he approached my car, I rolled down the window, wondering what was going on.

"Please don't tell your mother that Debbie came to lunch with us in Eau Claire," he said.

"Seriously?" I responded.

"Yes, she wouldn't understand, and it would just cause a lot of trouble for both of us."

I agreed, but as he drove away, I wondered how long he had been waiting for me alongside the road. It was dark outside, and he was on his way to the reformatory. How could someone as amazing as him be so afraid of his wife? I kept quiet and didn't talk about Dad's visit to Eau Claire.

Inspired by my father's career and my own interest in helping people, I started exploring the possibility of changing my major from art to social work. That summer between my sophomore and junior year I told my mother about my decision to switch majors. Her reaction was visceral, she started yelling at me that I was being foolish to change majors this late, and that I was throwing my college education away. As I sat in the recliner trying to explain, she suddenly got up from her chair and started punching me with her fists in my head. I instinctively covered my face with my arms and tried to kick her away from me.

When the recliner fell backwards onto the floor, I was on my back, but she continued to hit me. I was horrified and began to fear for my life. I pushed her away with my feet so I could get out from under her. When I did, I ran out of the house and jumped into my car. As I drove, I could feel eleven bumps forming on my skull, plus my face was cut and bruised. I couldn't believe what had just happened.

Bewildered and scared I drove to a friend's house. I asked if I could stay for the night. I was so ashamed and confused as to why she would do this to me. Why did she get so angry with me for switching my major from art to social work? I was doing it because I wanted to help people; why would she get mad at me for that? I was a dedicated student, and I could still finish school within four years.

The next morning, I saw my father's truck driving back and forth in front of my friend's house. He saw my car parked in the driveway. I went outside to talk to him. He was clearly upset and shaken by what he had heard when he got home from work that morning. He said he wanted me to come home. I told him that I was afraid of my own mother and couldn't understand how she could hurt me like that.

My father told me very quietly, "There are a lot of things you don't understand and probably never will. My advice is don't push it and come home."

I asked my father if he would ever leave my mother.

He said, "I would never leave her. It goes against my Catholic faith, and I take the oath of marriage very seriously."

I reluctantly followed my father's truck back to the house. My mother didn't say a word to me for two weeks.

I started my junior year by declaring my major in social work with a criminal justice emphasis and an art minor. This was an accredited BSW program.

I needed to fulfill 75-credits specific to social work to become licensed. I was committed to graduating in the remaining two years, and planned to take as many credits as I could. I wanted my mother to believe in me and be proud of me for graduating in four years.

One evening, in my non-verbal communications class, we were instructed to sit in front of a mirror with a small candle on our left. We gazed into a mirror with the lights turned off. Before we began, we were asked to form a question in our mind. I thought of being adopted and my birth mother and wondered what had happened and why she didn't want me. When I gazed into the mirror, I allowed my eyes to soften and saw a brick wall. Then I saw a woman climbing over the wall and running away. I was startled and confused by this insight. I immediately equated it with Nazi Germany, but knew I was born nine years after the concentration camps had been liberated. I wondered if my mother had been imprisoned, but for what?

That fall Debbie and I began volunteering at the Eau Claire free clinic. It was 1974; the Vietnam War was over, and the women's movement was moving forward. Birth control had only been legal for married women since 1965. In 1972 the Supreme Court ruled that it was now legal for unmarried people as well. 1973 also saw the passing of Roe vs Wade, but abortions were still illegal in Wisconsin.

When women came into the free clinic with an unexpected pregnancy, we always encouraged her to keep the baby or give it up for adoption. But, if she was convinced that neither of those options were possible, we referred her to Minnesota where abortions were safe and legal. I couldn't imagine women not having this choice or having access to a safe resource during this traumatic time in their life.

I believed strongly in a woman's right to choose what was right for her body and soul. I began learning about women's health issues and various forms of birth control, something I was very naïve about. My mother never had "the talk" with me. Instead, she put the "fear of God" in me.

Almost every college person I knew was in some type of relationship, except me. I had trust issues and had not made peace with my body. In fact, I was often called a prude by my college friends, especially Debbie.

Debbie and I now lived off campus, and I was feeling the freedom that came with having my own space. I wanted to explore and understand what everyone was talking about. My curiosity and my confidence had grown to the point that I starting taking the pill "just in case."

By the spring of 1975 I found myself in a relationship with someone I met through friends. He was kind and smart. Three months later I was terrified to discover that I was pregnant, even though I was on the pill. Only one percent of women became pregnant while taking the pill.

I was now 20 years old, enrolled in three summer school classes, plus working at Northern Colony. I had accepted two internships plus a full load of classes my senior year. I was planning to graduate in nine months. I didn't want to be a mother. I feared all of the decisions and consequences that were now in front of me. My first thought was of my mother Gertrude. I knew she would be furious with me, and I couldn't bear the shame, blame and guilt I would feel. I was fearful of what she would do to me physically and emotionally. When I imagined telling her that I was pregnant, all I could see was rage and fury. I didn't want to experience her anger and physical abuse again. I also knew I couldn't give a baby up for adoption. This was complicated by my unresolved feelings about my own adoption and all the confusion and secrecy that came with it.

Ashamed and confused, I searched my soul and weighed all of my options. My boyfriend was supportive of whatever decision I made. I could tell it was hard on him as I spiraled inward. I ended our relationship because I was ashamed and afraid. I didn't deserve to be loved by anyone.

It was ironic that I was a counselor who helped others make this very tough choice, and now I was right in the middle of it. I felt the gut-wrenching heartbreak of what this decision meant, but I also felt it was my only choice.

I scheduled my own appointment at the Meadowbrook Clinic in Minneapolis. A girlfriend drove me to the clinic on a hot, rainy day. When I arrived, I walked into a waiting room filled with women much older than I. I had expected to see younger women, but these were mature women with husbands and children sitting by their side. I could sense they all had their reasons and all of them carried the personal burden and pain of their decision. I could see in their faces how difficult this situation was for each of them. My friend waited for me in her car, and then drove me back to my apartment in Eau Claire. I was in a lot of pain, physically and emotionally. Everything was a blur.

Three days later I found myself wanting to be home. I wasn't going to tell my mother what had happened, I just wanted to be home and feel normal. My first evening after I arrived home, I was sitting in the living room contemplating what had just happened; to my body, my soul and my life.

I was just beginning to feel safe in my skin when I saw my mother charging toward me. She was standing in front of me holding my birth control pills in one hand and a manila envelope in the other yelling, "Now I have proof! I knew I never should have adopted you! You were a bad seed! I knew you would turn out to be just like your mother: a no-good, drunken prostitute!"

She threw the envelope at my chest and said, "Here, you've always wanted to know who your real mother is. Well here is your chance. Now you can see where you really come from! You're just like her!" She turned away, threw my pills on the floor and left the room.

Unbeknownst to me, my mother had been searching through my suitcase looking for birth control pills ever since my freshmen year!

I was now in a state of shock. My heart was racing. Yet, here were the answers to the questions I had been asking for years. This 9" x 12" manila envelope contained the truth about where I born and who my mother was. I was hesitant to open it. What if I was a bad seed, and my birth mother was everything Gertrude said she was? Was I going to end up just like her, or was I already just like her? Or even worse, would it prove I was related to Hitler or someone from the Holocaust?

With great trepidation I opened the envelope and discovered it was all written in German. I couldn't understand a word, except that my birth name was Carmen Sylvia and my birth mother's name was Karin. I quickly put it all back into the envelope and held it close to my pounding heart. I knew that when I was ready to find out more, I could.

I sat there clutching the envelope wondering how twisted this all was. If my mother Gertrude was this mad at me for just finding birth control pills, what would she have done to me if I had told her I was pregnant or worse yet, had an abortion?

Even though this was a cruel way to find out who my birth mother was, I also began to feel my birth mother's pain, along with a deep intuitive connection to her soul. Not only did I now know her name, but I also began to sense her spirit. I felt she had been victimized somehow. I remembered the vision in class of her in prison and climbing a wall.

Ironically Gertrude's reaction confirmed that I had made the right decision. I couldn't imagine the pain and anger this would have triggered in her if she knew the entire truth. I hated that I had to keep this a secret and the guilt I felt. I sensed that this wound within my mother, regarding my birth mother and me, was so dark and so deep that she could never, ever look at it.

That night I grieved for both of my mothers, as well as myself. I felt connected to the pain of being a woman based on this singular responsibility we all share.

In the middle of my senior year, I began having episodes of dizziness. As it turned out my wisdom teeth were wrapped around the central nerve in my face. I had to go to the hospital for surgery to reduce the risk of developing Bell's Palsy. I stayed there for four days. The doctors performed EEGs, EKGs, brain scans, and other related tests as benchmarks before and after the surgery. My mother didn't visit me. Our relationship was very strained and distant. On the day I was discharged, my doctor made an appointment for me to see a neurosurgeon.

A week later, I was in the neurosurgeon's office being greeted by an Indian doctor who asked me if I had extrasensory perception (ESP). I was shocked. I thought of my experiences and replied, "Yes." He told me that the tests showed that my brain waves were abnormal and they were similar to people with ESP or a heightened "sixth sense." He wanted me to go to St. Paul for further testing, because they were conducting a benchmark study regarding this exact phenomenon. He said that a part of my brain wasn't shutting down when I slept, which also meant that I probably had a lot of lucid dreams, which I did.

He said I would need my parents' permission, since I was under their health insurance.

The following week, I went home to ask my mother if I could go to St. Paul and be a part of this study group. She became so agitated by my request and accused me of creating drama where there didn't need to be any. She grabbed a large kitchen knife and held it above my head threatening to kill me because I was driving her crazy.

Luckily my father was home so I screamed as loud as I could. He ran into the kitchen and grabbed her hand.

He yelled, "Gertrude, what the hell are you doing?!"

I did not go to St. Paul.

CHAPTER 6: MOVING ON

In May 1976, I received my BSW. My mother came to the graduation ceremony, but not my father or brother. She stood outside the auditorium after the ceremony, but instead of congratulating me, she reminded me that I didn't graduate in four years because I took summer classes between my junior and senior year. The pain of her disapproval hurt deeply. She didn't want to go out for lunch, she didn't give me a card, and she left right after we talked on the sidewalk. I wondered if her goal was to humiliate me in person. What I felt was a major achievement seemed like a failure to her. My hope of her feeling proud of me was non-existent.

I saw my fellow students being hugged by family members and given flowers etc... I stood alone in a sea of love and victory when Paul, Wendy's old boyfriend whisked me up by the waist and twirled me around in the wind.

"We made it Laural, we made it!" he shouted. Indeed, we had; I was so grateful for his presence in my life.

The next day I went back to work. It was my second summer working as a recreational aide at Northern Colony near Chippewa Falls, Wisconsin. This was a self-contained, institutional community for severely and profoundly developmentally disabled children and adults who were now wards of the state. My time spent at the colony was totally life altering. I came to appreciate the idiosyncrasies, beauty and personalities of its residents. It was eye-opening to witness first-hand how they handled the immense physical, intellectual and emotional challenges they faced every day.

I worked with two Native American men from northern Wisconsin. Like me, they were college students at Eau Claire working here for the summer.

We became close friends through long discussions of their culture and traditions of honoring Mother Earth and Father Sky. The stories they shared of their customs and beliefs resonated within me. They also shared their hurt and resentment of living on reservation land with limited resources. Their wounds were fresh and their pain was etched in their faces.

They invited me to visit their reservation on the 4th of July, 1976 – America's Bicentennial. As we drove to the Lac Courte Oreilles reservation I was reminded of the beauty of this densely forested region. Large pine trees, rolling hills and clear freshwater lakes flowed past my window. When we entered the village center, I felt the energy shift as homemade signs regarding tribal hunting and fishing rights appeared in people's yards and public buildings. Their struggle was palpable as they were trying to protect this part of themselves. It was ironic to celebrate this country's Independence Day while witnessing how its original people had lost theirs.

I reflected on the land that Holzhausen Park stood on and how nature had inspired every culture's creation story. People throughout the world once felt interconnected with nature until Christianity declared all nature-based beliefs as "pagan." It's sad that the word "pagan," meaning "country dweller," was contorted into something evil that came to be feared, when nature actually inspired all the names of "god."

In August, I joined VISTA (Volunteers in Service to America), the domestic version of the Peace Corps. I had requested to be placed on an Indian reservation. Instead, my assignment was to work with inner-city children at the Longview Housing District in Decatur, Illinois. My job was to develop programs that would improve their self-esteem during a time of desegregation. I was nervous because I didn't really know Decatur or what I was getting into.

It was the fall of 1976. Decatur was a racially divided town that had just integrated their schools. It was a farming and manufacturing community located in the center of Illinois. Job opportunities had increased due to the growth of ADM (Archer Daniels Midland) and A.E. Staley. African American families had moved to Illinois from Alabama and Tennessee for work. Their presence wasn't totally embraced by the existing white community.

Being a young, white woman without a lot of urban experience, meant I had a lot to learn. My office was a basement room in an old brick house called the DOVE House. My first official assignment was a written test that assessed my ability to understand the words I would hear in the community I would be serving. I failed it miserably. I eventually learned their meanings so I could understand, but I didn't try to speak it. I wanted to be authentic and respect the culture I was walking into.

My next assignment was creating art programs for children and conversational rap sessions for teenagers. I went to visit the Longview Housing District, hoping to find a space for the art program. I introduced myself to the custodian who showed me a small community room that I could use. When I asked him where I could store art supplies, he graciously offered to share space with me in his janitor's closet. He even gave me a key, for which I was extremely grateful. He didn't need to trust me, but he did, and that was all I needed to get started.

I created posters and began putting them up around the neighborhood. Little by little, I collected donated materials from local hardware stores and art supply shops and began teaching a weekly arts and crafts class. A collection of old cigar boxes inspired my first art project.

To my delight ten children showed up and we made macaroni-covered treasure chests, sprayed with gold paint.

The harder assignment would be getting teenagers to talk about their feelings. I created a poster that announced Teen Night at the DOVE House. I pinned it up on the bulletin board at the community center. I nervously waited in the basement of the DOVE house that first night, wondering if anyone would show up. Six teenagers came as a group of close friends. There were two boys and four girls.

One of them asked, "So what is this all about?"

I said, "This is a place where you can feel free to talk about anything."

"Anything?" he replied.

"Yes," I responded.

He then asked me to describe an orgasm. I knew if I didn't, they would leave and I would lose them.

Fortunately, my years of working at the Eau Claire free clinic paid off. I wasn't afraid to talk about it and I knew how to do it without being vulgar or sugar-coated.

The teens were surprised and intrigued by my honesty. They began to open up as they sensed this was a safe place to express what was really going on in their minds. Soon the word got out that Teen Night at the DOVE House was for real, and attendance grew every week. Eventually we had over 50 teens attending on a regular basis.

A lot of what they shared focused on being excluded from extracurricular activities at their high school. I was genuinely shocked that their school would do that, so I asked more questions and wanted examples. They told me story after story of how they felt excluded or overlooked because of their skin color. No one wanted them in their groups.

It was clear that they really wanted to belong to something, so we brainstormed ideas that would inspire participation, creativity and pride.

After several months of meetings and discussion they said they wanted to create a community-wide talent show.

The younger children wanted to create a calendar that featured their drawings. It could be sold at the talent show. The teens wanted to focus on dance routines, skits and a fashion show. All proceeds would fund future DOVE House projects for their neighborhood.

I called a local television station to ask if they would be willing to do a segment to promote the talent show. They agreed and wanted to film one of our acts in their studio to promote the show. I talked with the parents and they all agreed to sign permission slips for their children to leave school, just for the filming. I talked to the teens who had decided on a dance number that six of them created. The station then scheduled the filming for the following week at 1:00 pm. Unfortunately, the school principal threatened to expel them all if they went. The teens came to me very upset. I told them I would to meet with the principal to explain. I made an appointment to see him the very next day.

He seemed cordial at first. I sat in a chair across from his desk as I began to explain how this was an excellent learning experience for them to see a television studio in action, how they would only be gone for one hour, and that it could boost their confidence and self-esteem as well as showcase the school.

Without any dialogue he abruptly stood up and said, "No, I've already decided, they will be expelled if they go."

I replied, "But you should be proud of them."

He pointed at me, "I don't need to listen to a bleeding-heart liberal like you." Then he pointed to the door and said, "I want you to leave this building now!"

As I stood, I said very clearly, "If you expel them for going, I will tell the truth of what you said. The television station has already booked the time and is expecting them."

He silently and sternly escorted me out the building, and we didn't say another word to each other.

I didn't want to make a scene in the school hallways and I sensed neither did he. When I got in my car I exhaled. I couldn't believe a narrow-minded individual like that was the principal of an integrated high school!

I met with the students and their parents to discuss our options. We decided to move forward as planned. It all went fine, no one was expelled, but it was the beginning of my education in racism and standing up for what is right.

A few days later, I received a phone call from a man who said he had heard about our program. Robert Fitch introduced himself as Martin Luther King's personal photographer. He wanted to photograph the children's art program. I was honored by his call and asked if he would be willing to speak to the class about his work. He agreed.

That week one of the teens from Teen Night introduced me to his older brother, a well-known local artist and DJ. His brother was a gentle soul who had been in a car accident, leaving him paralyzed from the waist down. He cared deeply for his community and wanted to offer his DJ services for the talent show. We became friends as we shared ideas and collaborated on the poster and other promotional materials.

The talent show happened in a local church auditorium to a standing-room-only crowd. It was a huge success. A few weeks later I invited my new friend for dinner to celebrate. His friends carried him up the steps in his wheelchair and left. We had a great time talking and sharing stories. After dinner he called his friends who came and carried him back down.

The following Monday, my white landlord, who had been trying to get me to come to church, knocked on my door and told me I was being evicted.

When I asked him why, he said it was because I had a black man in my apartment overnight. I tried to explain but he wouldn't listen. He told me that the two elderly white sisters who lived below had called him that weekend. They were afraid I was bringing in the "wrong type" of people.

I was furious and worried about where I would live. As a VISTA volunteer you are given a very small stipend, and affordable housing was hard to find. Since arriving in Decatur, I had moved three times in nine months. I started out in a large communal home with all the VISTA volunteers as a "trial period." Then I moved in with a married couple, but that didn't work out, so I was thrilled when I found this upstairs studio apartment. Now I had to look again.

To ground myself I joined a yoga class at the YMCA. Our instructor taught us how to breathe and connect with our energy body or chakras. This was my first introduction to Eastern philosophy and I was amazed by the calm it gave me. During this time, I was also volunteering at the Decatur Planned Parenthood Clinic. One of the doctors noticed that I looked pale and asked me if I was okay. I told him that my heart was racing a lot and I felt tingly. I had chalked it up to all the stress and my current living dilemma. He did a quick physical and listened to my heart. He encouraged me to see a heart specialist in Chicago at Loyola University. He set me up with Dr. Scanlan on June 3 as a gift for my hard work. Dr. Scanlan put me through a series of tests. His diagnosis was that I had a congenital heart defect. He said it was worsening due to stress and asthma. He felt I needed to leave Decatur and go home to rest. I resisted because I only had two months left in my contract. He was quite persuasive and explained that I was jeopardizing my health.

This was a hard decision; I didn't want to leave now.

When I returned to Decatur, I reviewed the pros and cons. The pros were that I had accomplished quite a bit in a short period of time. There were now volunteers in place to continue the arts program along with dedicated funding, supplies and staffing to open three locations. The teens were assimilating at school and seemed more confident and determined to succeed. The biggest con was my guilt for leaving early and that I had the choice to leave.

I was very aware of how fortunate I was that I had choices. I didn't take that lightly. But I knew I needed to take care of myself. I turned in my resignation, packed up my stuff and drove myself home.

I moved back to my parents' house, something I never thought I would do. I wanted to try and heal my relationship with my mother. She had a heart attack and was diagnosed with type II diabetes. Her health was failing and I sensed she could use my company.

Soon after I settled in, a position opened up as the Developmental Disabilities Counselor Coordinator at the Unified Board in Kewaunee County. It was a long shot, but I sent in my resume. I was invited in for an interview even though the position required a Masters of Social Work. The interview went very well, and by the next day I was offered the job! They felt that my experience, combined with the fact that I was a licensed social worker with a BSW, fulfilled the job requirements. I jumped around my parents' kitchen yelling with joy, my mom even joined in. I could see that she was truly proud of me for the first time in my life.

The majority of my job was focused on the needs of the developmentally disabled. This included home-training for children 0-3, along with programs for developmentally disabled adults 18+ throughout Kewaunee County.

I also counseled parents who struggled with tough decisions regarding how to care for their children, especially as they got older. I helped to create the first community-based residential facility (CBRF) in our area.

Since I was the only female counselor at the Unified Board, I was given the opportunity to become a family and marriage counselor. I attended programs that were certified in family counseling, drug and alcohol counseling as well as sex and marriage counseling. I was supervised by our staff psychiatrist and psychologist, who trained me in the assessment of mental illness. There were four total counselors in our office. We rotated one week a month to be on 24-hour call to handle crisis situations. We assisted local law enforcement to help them assess and intervene on calls that involved suicide attempts, family violence, drug or alcohol overdoses, psychotic outbreaks, etc...

Being a crisis counselor in the same rural community I had grown up in was sometimes too close for comfort; I was dealing with situations involving friends, family, neighbors, and parents of friends. This new perspective into our community and all of its challenges helped me understand my mother as a businesswoman and community activist. I was determined to spend more quality time with her so we could heal the wounds between us.

Her Lutheran faith meant a lot to her. She invited me to attend Christmas Eve Mass at her church. I had not been in a church except for funerals. I was expecting to share a beautiful sweet evening together, but her pastor began preaching that Jews, Muslims, or anyone who didn't accept Jesus as their lord and savior would burn in hell. I felt my stomach turn. I couldn't believe he was preaching this on Christmas Eve! I told my mother I had to leave. She didn't want me to make a scene.

I told her that I couldn't sit and listen to this. I felt that if I stayed, it meant I was agreeing to it, which made me a hypocrite. I quietly stood up and walked out. I waited in the car until the service was over. My mom was not happy with me, but she didn't get mad at me either. I never went back to her church again.

A few weeks later, my mom's pastor made an appointment to see me. When I saw him on my schedule, I thought maybe he needed some personal help. Instead, he came in to try to talk me into coming back to church. When I told him why I left, he damned me to hell, in my office!

This only solidified my decision to stay away. I found myself searching for answers regarding my faith and what I perceived to be Jesus's teachings versus the doctrine of the Lutheran or Catholic Church. I had heard about a pastor at the Community Congregational Church in Kewaunee, so I set up a time to meet with him. I immediately felt safe with him and began sharing my encounters with the Tree Spirit and my thoughts on Jesus. He felt that I had been "called" to teach, which sounded very odd to me at the time.

A year later, that same pastor asked me if I would set up a Planned Parenthood clinic in our community. He was concerned about the high rate of teen pregnancy and was hoping I could help. What a contrast! To be damned to hell by one minister, yet asked by another to open a Planned Parenthood clinic. Life was truly unpredictable.

I pondered his request because I was beginning to question my position at the Unified Board. I was working very long hours, doing the work of three people. My caseload was growing and sessions were now limited to 50 minutes each. I was being encouraged to support the use of anti-anxiety and anti-depressant medications for people dealing with trauma or situational depression, which was something I didn't totally agree with.

Disillusioned with my job, I accepted the challenge. I resigned my position at the Unified Board, left the security of a steady paycheck with insurance benefits, to jump headfirst into the world of non-profit and community healthcare. Ironically, two full-time and one part-time positions were created to replace me, but I didn't look back.

I began the process of applying for a grant to open the first Planned Parenthood Clinic in Kewaunee County. I talked with several doctors in the area to see if they would be interested in volunteering their services until we had the funding to pay them. Fortunately, I found a family practice doctor who was glad to be of service. His support helped me secure the grant we needed to move forward. Within months I had secured a space, several exam tables, medical supplies and office furniture. My desire was to create a safe place for women to receive quality healthcare, education, and resources for themselves and their family. We opened the clinic in 1979.

During this time, I married a man from Chicago. We had been living together for almost two years. Shortly after our wedding we learned that he needed surgery on both knees, due to years of juvenile arthritis. Neither of us had health insurance. It was ironic to be the executive director of a women's health clinic and be without health insurance. The only option I had was to turn the clinic over to my friend Chris and find a job with benefits. It was a very difficult decision. I remember the clinic's doctor asking, "How can you leave your brainchild?" But I did.

The only job with immediate family health insurance was a position as an extended care caseworker at Curative Workshop in Green Bay. I accepted the position along with a case-load of over 50 long-term clients. I juggled my new job, as John went through knee surgery and rehab. After his surgery, he withdrew and our marriage disintegrated.

John was a brilliant man, but he had tested fate by taking jobs that required intense amounts of physical labor, something he could no longer do. I contacted the director of vocational rehab and asked if he would be willing to evaluate John as a potential client. John met with him and took a battery of tests. I received a phone call from the director who confirmed John's high intelligence. He was immediately approved to receive college assistance, which would help him transition from a laborer into a professional career. John had been a brilliant computer programmer in Chicago in the 60s. Now he could embrace that part of himself and attend UWGB in fall. I was excited for him.

A few days later I was called into the director's office at Curative Workshop and fired for insubordination without any warning! I asked why, and I was told that my supervisor had requested it and that I had to leave immediately. I sensed this was connected to an incident when I had questioned my supervisor in private about telling inappropriate sexual jokes in front of our clients, especially since one was a known sex offender who could be triggered. I was shocked!

With our life at a crossroads, John and I agreed to go our separate ways. I filed for a pro-se divorce and moved on.

I was now without a job, a home or a life partner.

I thought about going back to the clinic, but Chris had everything under control and there wasn't enough funding to support both of us.

I had no choice but to move in with my parents. I felt like a failure on every possible level. I began suffering severe panic attacks. The left side of my body would go numb; I thought I was having heart attacks. My sleep was disrupted by night terrors. In one of the dreams, a face split in half, was lying on the tarmac of an airfield. One side was trying to talk to the other side, which wasn't responding.

I bent down and held the two sides in my hands and put them together so they could feel whole. As they came together they formed the shape of a heart. Even though they were dying, there was love. I realized the faces represented the separation and longing I felt within me.

I had been seeing a psychologist who diagnosed me with PTSD (Post Traumatic Stress Disorder) and (PSSD Psycho-Somatic Stress Disorder), which meant my stress was making me sick. I opened up to him about the Tree Spirit, and wondered if he might think I was delusional. On the contrary; he thought I was a totally rational woman with a difficult story. I saw him session after session and talked about my relationship with my mother, my adoption and my abortion. I told him about the bullying and my feelings of guilt, confusion and loss. He asked me if I ever got angry.

I said, "No, not really. I try to rise above anger because I can see how hurt other people are."

He said my thinking was a way to escape feeling the emotions I suppressed. He explained that I was like someone who had a life ring from a sinking ship. When I saw people drowning, I gave them my life ring, but I was hurt because no one gave me theirs or tried to save me.

I was agitated by his analogy and told him that it was ridiculous. He continued to defend his thinking. I felt a swell of emotions flood through me as I became so angry that I yelled at him and said I was never going back. This was one of the first times in my life I ever expressed anger to someone out loud. I also never went back, but I appreciated what he was telling me.

My heart really wanted to go back to school to finish my original art major. I set up a meeting with a few art faculty members to review my art portfolio. I was immediately accepted into the arts program at UWGB.

*"Love is like a tree, it grows of its own accord,
it puts down deep roots into our whole being."*
- Victor Hugo -

CHAPTER 7: STARTING OVER

It felt great to be a student again. I loved the excitement of learning and meeting new people. Since I already had a bachelor's degree with an art minor, I only needed to take art courses to earn a second degree! This meant that I could express myself freely and experiment with new ideas that allowed me to reconnect with my creativity.

That first semester as an art student was a blur due to the fact that I was also filing divorce papers, appearing in court and moving into an apartment in Green Bay on my own. My parents were upset with me for getting divorced, leaving my job and getting fired in the same year. I filed for housing allowance, food stamps and financial aid to survive.

At the beginning of my second semester, someone asked me if I ever wanted to get married again. I emphatically said "no way." She continued to pry until I answered, "Only if he were the perfect guy." She asked me to describe "the perfect guy." I played along: he would be 6'2" with broad shoulders and dark hair. He would have glasses, a mustache and dark eyes. He needed to be sensitive yet strong, and be a combination of a carpenter and an artist. He would want to live in the country and have a passion for art, nature, peace and trees. My friend looked at me and said I was being too choosy. I replied, "Not really; if I'm ever getting married again that's what I want."

Later that day, as I was settling into modern art history class, I noticed a guy walk in who took my breath away. The following day, he showed up in my studio arts sculpture class too! Eventually I worked up the courage to ask him to join me in the commons for coffee.

He did, and we talked for hours. I learned that Paul was a union carpenter who was studying to become an oil painter. He was sensitive yet strong. He was 6'2" with broad shoulders. His hair was dark; he had hazel eyes, a mustache and wore glasses. The similarities to the description of my "perfect man" were so striking it freaked me out a bit. Paul invited me to a jazz concert at the Blue Whale Coffee House later that night. I immediately said, "Sure!"

But when I got home, I got scared and didn't go. The whole concept terrified me. It was too fast and too soon. We barely made eye contact with each other the next week as I realized I had blown it.

That Friday, he called and asked me if I would ever go out with him.

I said, "Yes."

He said, "Okay," and hung up.

I waited all weekend for him to call me back. Several days later, in art history class I invited him to study at my apartment. He agreed and came over. We studied for a few hours, but it was such a beautiful spring day in March, that we decided to go for a ride in the country in his 1971 green Volvo. Inside, a carefully placed bottle of champagne and two glasses were perched between the seats. We drove hours along wooded roads and parks throughout the country and talked the entire time. We discovered how much we had in common. Paul revealed that he had been attracted to me since the first day in art history class but that he was too afraid to get involved in a relationship. I told him I felt the same way. Eventually he moved in with me.

Six months later, his father Roger showed up at our apartment. Roger was a traditional man who worked at the same paper mill in Green Bay all his life.

He asked us if we were going to get married Paul and I looked at each other with fear and anticipation.

His father pushed us a bit more; he wanted a date. My heart started pounding. It was a very surreal experience that Paul and I were making this huge decision in front of his father and in this exact moment. This wasn't a proposal, it was an ultimatum.

We simultaneously said "yes."

After his father left, I thought of my parents and what their reaction might be. I knew they weren't happy with me. I asked Paul if he would ask my parents, since it was his father who started this. He agreed. He went to Algoma for dinner and asked them if he could marry me. He told them he loved me and wanted to spend the rest of his life with me. Apparently, they warned Paul that I was "all used up" but if he was okay with that they wouldn't stand in our way.

Paul and I were married January 30th, 1982, on a snowy Sunday evening. We held the entire event at the Blue Whale Coffee House, the very place where I stood him up nine months earlier. It was perfect for us. My parents told us they wouldn't come if I invited anyone from my previous wedding. This hurt us both, but we wanted them there. Our wedding was intimate with fewer than fifty family and friends.

Our wedding January 30th, 1982 in the Blue Whale Coffee House at UWGB.

We said our vows in front of a warm, glowing fireplace, and our dear friends Lee and Jim played folk music all evening. Everyone wore jeans as we requested.

Paul and I splurged for a champagne fountain filled with the same French champagne we shared on our first date.

Four months after our wedding my father was diagnosed with inoperable colon cancer. The day after his surgery I visited him in the hospital. His advice was, "Don't work as hard as I did; take your vacation days, and enjoy your life. Work is not all that it's cracked up to be, Peaches. Please...do this for me."

I had interviewed for a job a few weeks before graduation and immediately started working as a graphic artist on the Monday after the ceremony. I graduated in May 1982, with a Bachelor's degree in communication arts. No one came to the ceremony except for Paul. It wasn't a joyous occasion, for my father was dying.

I visited my father at the hospital every night after work. We talked about Germany and he told me that the headquarters for his CIA unit were in our home. My mind flashed on the attic filled with film equipment. When I asked him about that, he told me that mom worked for him as the office clerk and photo processor. It all began to make a little bit more sense to me. I asked him why we left Germany. He told me that his cover had been blown and his office was shut down; that we had no choice but to leave right away.

He explained that we left in November of 1961, after the Cold War standoff, known as the Berlin Crisis, between the United States and the Soviet Union. He didn't have anything nice to say about Russia as he murmured under his breath. When the Iron Curtain was built it effectively separated East Germany from West Germany. When I asked him how his cover was blown, he told me he couldn't answer that. I asked him if he could tell me anything about my adoption, he said "no". The conversation ended abruptly as he lowered his eyes and grabbed my arm.

I told him I loved him.

He gently squeezed my arm, and then let go. My father lapsed into a coma and died four days later, on June 25th, 1982 – the exact day he was scheduled to retire.

For his retirement, Dad had been looking forward to buying land in the country and raising horses. My father had sacrificed so much during his life and asked for very little in return. He had accrued 350 unused vacation days, but never used them.

My father John Virtues.

My mother wasn't able to arrange a proper Catholic funeral as he requested. My father was dedicated to his faith, but because of his schedule he attended Catholic Mass in Green Bay right after his Sunday morning shift. When my mother asked the Catholic church in Algoma if they would officiate, they refused because he wasn't an official member. She asked the church in Green Bay, where my father attended, and they also refused. As it turned out, Catholics at that time could only be a member of the church in their immediate home area, but because he didn't attend the Algoma church, they couldn't bury him.

It didn't seem fair and it caused a lot of pain at a very tragic time. After all his years of dedication and service to his God and his country, my father was laid to rest in a funeral home with a Lutheran minister who didn't know him. I was so mad at the world and the Catholic Church for not treating him with the love and respect he deserved.

An American flag was draped over his casket, but my mother refused to have a full, military funeral. She was so angry at the world that she wasn't thinking clearly. My parents had not made out a will or bought a cemetery plot. When I asked her what we were going to do with my father's ashes, she said, "His ashes can end up in the landfill for all I care." I was shocked, so I asked if I could have his ashes. She said, "Fine, do with them what you want."

A week later, Paul and I scattered his ashes in a horse pasture in the country near Sugar Bush, Wisconsin. I knew that my father's dream was to live on a ranch with horses. For now, this was the best I could do to honor that dream.

A month later, my mother handed me four, large three-ring binders filled with official records.

I asked her what they were.

She said, "Laural, it's time for you to have this. These are our official records from Germany, including your original adoption papers. There is a binder for you, one for your father, one for me, and one for your brother. Now that your father is gone, you can read this."

These binders were filled with government documents, passports, and letters from the European Command Center and the CIA. I wanted to learn more about my father, so I read his binder first. There were letters of recommendation about his performance and even a copy of the requisition form used to secure our home near Holzhausen Park so it could function as his unit's headquarters. There was a resume that outlined how he specialized in conducting investigations and surveillance of "indigenous personnel."

This meant that my father was spying on spies; Germans that were recruited to help the United States battle Russia during the Cold War.

It was fascinating and I wished I could talk to him about all of this. I had so many questions so I asked my mother. She confirmed for the first time that she was the office clerk and film developer, and that the attic was her photo lab. She also told me where their office was in the house. Wow! Both of my parents had operated undercover for the CIC and the CIA from 1948-61.

I reflected on what an adjustment it must have been for both of them. My father went from being in charge of a CIA unit in Frankfurt to being a prison guard in Green Bay. Some things began to make sense to me, yet other things didn't make any sense at all. My heart felt heavier as I grieved for all he and my mother had lost.

Mom became more dependent on me after Dad died. Even with all her irrational outbursts and abuse, I still loved her. I could see how alone and vulnerable she was.

Paul and I decided to buy a 180-year-old vertical log home in the country. He was still taking classes at UWGB and working fulltime for Orde, an outdoor sign company. A year after our marriage, we learned that I was pregnant. I was excited and nervous. I drove to Algoma to tell my mother the good news. She wasn't happy that I would want to bring a child into this horrible, cruel world. She said I was being selfish, and that no child deserved the fate this world would give it. I was shocked and saddened by her reaction.

I knew deep inside it was her own pain of not having children that she was expressing.

I told her point-blank, "Mom, I can't accept that life is that hopeless. I have to believe that my child will help to make this world a better place. I am going to have this baby with that intent." I was determined that my baby would be treated with complete and unconditional love.

77

During my pregnancy, my doctor told me to leave my job at the printing shop because of the ink fumes.

Fortunately, I had the opportunity to work with Paul and our friend Timothy at the Neville Public Museum. The Museum had just moved into a new building and we were being asked to install all of its artifacts into the new permanent exhibit called The Edge of the Inland Sea.

It was fascinating to hold hundreds of ancient artifacts in my hands and connect with the history of each one. I learned that after the last Ice Age, a group of Paleo-Indian hunter-gatherers lived in here between 10,000-6000 BCE. They hunted mastodons and giant bison with these exact stone tools. As I held each piece, I studied its age and what its purpose was. I sensed the energy of how it was used.

The later pottery shards especially intrigued me. I imagined herbs, tree saps and nuts they once held. I honored and thanked each piece before placing it onto the display board and securing it with sterling silver before it was encased in glass. The idea that my hands were the last hands to touch these ancient artifacts was both humbling and sacred. It was profound to share this experience with the child that was growing within me.

Our son, Tyler, was born on February 29th, 1984 – coincidentally, my mother Gertrude's 64th birthday. It was amazing that her only grandchild was born on her birthday, and that they now shared a leap-year birthday made it even more amazing. I felt blessed to be able to give her this gift. Even though Tyler was not her blood, he was spiritually connected to her in a very unique way. It was about as close to having a biological grandchild as she could experience.

Having Tyler baptized was very important to my mother, so he was baptized at the Lutheran church near our home in Wayside on April Fool's Day, 1984.

The Pastor of this church had a broader perspective of Christianity that made me feel more comfortable. It was okay with him that Paul was baptized a Catholic; it was okay that Paul and I had been married ecumenically and that I was divorced. Tyler qualified to be baptized here because I had been confirmed in the Lutheran faith. It was all for Mom.

Tyler was a godsend. He brought so much love into my mother's heart that allowed her to begin healing her anger. That Christmas, she gave me a crystal ornament of a ballerina in a pirouette pose; she wanted me to know how proud she was of me. At the time I was the president of the Wisconsin Ballet Theater and the vice president/creative director at Media Management Inc. Her gift meant so much to me because we were beginning to recognize the eccentric yet driven souls within each of us.

That summer, my mother went to Florida by herself to begin a new life. She drove her RV to a trailer park filled with retirees in Panama City, Florida. She began meeting new people and making new friends.

Paul and I flew down to visit, and we brought Tyler so she could introduce him to her camp mates. As usual, she was organizing events and giving orders. We attended a party held in our honor in a large common area. Mom and I danced together for the first time and we were having fun. She was in her element; everyone there loved her.

Four months later I received a phone call that shook me to the core. Apparently, my mother had gone in to see a doctor the day before and had given him my name as her emergency contact. He was now explaining to me that she had less than two years to live. He told me that she had congestive heart failure and an incurable form of leukemia that was complicated by her Type 2 Diabetes. I couldn't believe what I was hearing.

He told me that he wasn't going to tell her what he was telling me. He felt that it would hurt her more than help her. He wanted me to know so I could be prepared. I agreed, for I didn't want to spoil the joy she was finally feeling.

After the conversation ended, I sat at my desk and sobbed. This felt like a repeat of getting the prognosis for my father all over again. She was still in her sixties.

That spring, I took a week off of work to drive Mom and her trailer back to Wisconsin. The heat of a Florida summer was too much for her northern constitution. Plus, I was concerned about her making this drive by herself. She didn't quite understand why I wanted to do this for her. I told her it was so she and I could have a grand adventure together.

It was more than an adventure pulling a 28-foot 5th wheeler behind a Chevy Suburban for the first time. I marveled at the strength and endurance it took to maneuver a rig like this. I reflected on the fact that she had driven this all over the country. We shared a fondness for Willy Nelson and his song, *On the Road Again*. It became our theme song as I found myself admiring her more with every mile.

As we drove north to Chattanooga, Tennessee I saw a sign for Ruby Falls and Lookout Mountain. The sign said there was a huge waterfall deep inside a cave, in the middle of the mountain! I wanted to see this so I took the next exit off the interstate. I hadn't planned to drive up a very steep and curvy road pulling a trailer. When we finally reached the summit of Lookout Mountain, she was exhausted just watching me execute all the sharp turns. But we made it and I wanted to celebrate.

She was not so thrilled.

I could see that she was very pale and weak. She said, "You go Laural, you got us all the way up here, you go see what it's all about and then tell me about it."

The cave was amazing it felt very sacred yet familiar.

When the tour was over, we sat under a tree in the outdoor café and enjoyed lunch and lemonade while taking in the expansive view.

The next day, we drove to Nashville and took a riverboat dinner cruise on the Delta Queen. We were having fun getting to know each other.

We drove home the next day. She parked her trailer at our house so she could help us during the week by making meals. She wanted to spend as much time as she could with her precious grandson. Tyler was the perfect medicine for her.

In 1988 Tyler and Mom celebrated their first official leap-year birthday. They were each technically four years older, but in leap-year terms, it was only one year. I wanted to do something special because I knew that this would be the only leap-year birthday they would get to share together. So I called the local media. Soon a photographer from the *Green Bay Press-Gazette* came out and took a wonderful picture of the two of them.

Birthday greetings: Gertrude Virtues, Algoma, and grandson Tyler Wauters met for their Leap Year birthday party at the Wauters' southern Brown County home Sunday. Virtues was born on Feb. 29, 1920, and Tyler was born on Feb. 29, 1984.

Leap-Day babies jumping for joy over birthdays

Front-page story in the Green Bay Press Gazette. February 29th, 1988.

It ended up on the front page of the Sunday paper.

That fall, Mom stubbornly insisted on driving her trailer back to Florida by herself.

In spring she caravanned with her brother Arnie.

On her way home, Mom had a heart attack on the interstate. Paul and I got the call and drove to Danville, Illinois. We found her in the hospital needing a blood transfusion. I arranged for a Learjet to transport her home.

It was January 1989 and the sun was shining through the frosted windows. Mom was sitting on a chair in the sun when told me that she knew she was dying. She began to cry. She wanted to have more time to enjoy Tyler and watch him grow up. It was as if she were being given the opportunity to be a better parent. She told me how she believed in me, and that even though she had her doubts, I had proven her wrong. She was amazed at all the messes I had gotten myself into, yet I always came out smelling like a rose. I wondered if anyone ever told her she was a rose.

I asked her about her mother and she told me how hard her mother was on her - that she never felt supported being a career woman. Mom wanted to go to college and be a newspaper writer and editor, but her family believed that a woman's place was in the home. She felt her brothers got all the support and attention. She was also the middle child; life was hard and unfair. I could feel her sadness and her pain in not being honored for all she had accomplished in her life. She showed me her high-school yearbook and shared with me how she had started the first women's athletic club. She told me how her classmates thought she would become the dean of a prestigious college. I could see the reality of what her generation of women had to deal with and how hard she fought to be seen as an intelligent woman with leadership skills. In her eyes, my life was easy in comparison.

At the end of March, she was admitted into the hospital. I stayed with her until her passing on April 2nd, 1989. I asked Henry, to sprinkle Mom's ashes in the same horse pasture where we placed Dad's ashes. He agreed.

We didn't have a headstone or plaque to remember our parents by, just a field to gaze into. They had hoped to be buried in Arlington National Cemetery, but my mother told me they didn't qualify, so I didn't pursue it.

Later that year, on November 14, 1989, the Iron Curtain, also known as the Berlin Wall came down, ending 28 years of separation and pain. The Soviet Union was starting to crumble, and this wall was symbolic of that process. I was thrilled to see it finally come down, but I was deeply saddened that neither of my parents was alive.

We had left Germany so suddenly in 1961, the exact year the wall went up. I thought of all the emotions that wall represented. Now it was coming down and I couldn't share that moment with the only two people who understood me.

My first birthday without my mother was empty. Her absence had left a giant void in my life, which was compounded by the fact that now both of my parents were gone. Even though I was 35 years old and a mother, I still felt like a child on my birthday.

In that moment I received an anonymous phone call from an elderly woman with a German accent. I sensed it was from a payphone, because I heard the connection clicking in.

"Is this 864-2709?" the woman asked.

"Yes, it is," I replied.

"Sorry, this is the wrong number," and she hung up.

My heart stopped! I instantly felt that this call was directly connected to my birth mother. I wondered if this person knew that today was my birthday, and that both of my parents were now gone. Was I being watched? My whole body started to shake, and my mind began to race. How did this woman find me? Was she following me? But if so, why didn't she want to talk to me?

And how did this woman know where I lived when I didn't have a clue where she was? I thought of the envelope sitting in my closet upstairs that contained all of my adoption information.

83

When I was a counselor, I had portions of it interpreted by a coworker who knew some German. When he read it to me, I learned that my mother had spent time in jail after I was born, and that the man I thought was my father had the marriage annulled just weeks before my birth. It was such a sad story.

I was grieving the loss of the mother I had just grown to love. The thought of finding my birth mother was too overwhelming in that moment. I knew someday I would have the courage to act on it, but not yet.

One month later, Paul's father told us about a piece of property in foreclosure that we should see. We had just finished remodeling our old log home, and we were pretty exhausted from everything that had happened. But in spite of that, we drove by the house he had suggested. It was a cold January day with several feet of snow on the ground.

The property was engulfed in trees, and the driveway had not been plowed for some time. We stopped, and my heart stopped too. It was like looking at a winter wonderland. We got out of the car and began to walk around. We could see a pond on the right with an aerator; when we walked over to it, we also discovered a sauna! We walked to the end of the pond, and saw another pond behind an enormous two-story, pole building. We looked at each other and thought the same thing: It's perfect for an art studio and shop. We continued walking in the back even though the snow was up to our knees. We suddenly realized we were in the middle of a huge orchard of over 100 fruit trees, and on the other side was another pond! That pond was totally encircled by weeping willows trees.

To the south was a large stand of oak, pine, and cedar. We began to feel we were walking in a magical place.

It brought back memories of Holzhausen Park, Germany. For Paul, it looked like Monet's home in Giverny, France. This would be the perfect place to raise our son. I had always wanted to give Tyler the gift of being surrounded by nature, to create a lifetime of memories in a special, sacred space. This felt exactly like that type of space. Paul and I hugged each other and began to wonder if we could make this dream and reality.

We made an offer on the house that afternoon. By the next morning it was accepted! The bank set our closing date for February 28, 1990. This was the date we would have celebrated Tyler and Mom's birthday. I saw it as a blessing.

The closing day came, and we still had not sold our other home. We were at the bank signing the final papers when we got a call from our realtor. She told us she had just gotten a good offer on our log house. Upon hearing the news, I couldn't help but think that Mom and Dad had something to do with this, too. We accepted the offer, and moved out of the old house and into our new home.

The date was April 2. My mother had died exactly one year before on April 2, and now we were starting a new life in a new home. I love the synchronicity of life when it happens like this. There is so much comfort in it.

The day after we moved in, I went for a walk in the backyard. My goal was to sit on a large rock next to the back pond and relax, but I found I couldn't walk very far before I would have an anxiety attack. I told myself how foolish this was. Eventually, I made it to the rock and sat down. I was light-headed, and my heart was pounding. I took a couple of deep breaths and tried to focus on what I was feeling. Looking at the pond in front of me, I felt overwhelmed by its beauty. I reflected on how this land was bigger than us.

It had been here before us and would continue on after we were gone.

Then it dawned on me that we didn't own this land; we only bought the rights to take care of it. What a relief this revelation was to me. My anxiety stopped.

During this time, I also made the difficult decision to leave the agency I had helped build. I wasn't feeling very appreciated and tensions were rising between me and the three male partners. At one point, during my review, the majority owner asked me what Paul would think if I made more money than he did, since I was a woman. I was offended by his question and began to realize that this may be a dead end for me. At the time, I was being recruited by investors to open my own agency and by another agency to help them expand. The other agency, Goltz and Associates, was owned by Bob Goltz. He was the person responsible for creating the graphic arts department at UWGB and had been a mentor to me as a student. His agency had a stellar reputation for creative excellence. I was excited to join him and his team. It was a difficult transition, as I was torn between leaving the agency I helped to birth and to rebuild another agency with a staff I didn't know. But I did it.

In late November 1993, Paul and I received a message from the *Green Bay Press-Gazette*. They wanted to do a story on how we, as a young family, juggled two full-time jobs, a freelance business and managed forty acres of farmland. I think this came up because Paul and I had just taken on the creation and building of a multi-dimensional educational exhibit that Bob Goltz passed on to us. Its focus was improving the water quality of the Fox River. When the photographer came to our house to interview us and take pictures, I instantly recognized him. He was the same photographer who had taken the photos of Tyler and Mom on their leap-year birthday, and today was my birthday.

With teary eyes, I thanked him for the wonderful photo and told him how my mother had died the following year and how his photo honored the special bond they had. As we talked, he asked, "Where were you born?"

"I was born in Germany but I was adopted," I said.

He shared that he had just come back from Germany and that his entire family was German. Then he asked, "Have you ever thought of finding your birth parents?"

I said, "I have thought about it, but it never felt right." He told me that if I waited too long, my birth parents might not be alive. In that moment I realized I had just received the permission I needed to begin my search. The man who had photographed my mother and Tyler on their first and only official leap-year birthday, was now photographing Paul, Tyler, and me on my birthday. This was truly a sign.

When New Year's Day 1994 began, I declared that this was the year I was going to find my birth mother. I even wrote my intention in my journal and drew a tree next to it in honor of the Tree Spirit. My journal has always been a touchstone for me throughout my life. I didn't write in it every day, but when something important happened, I liked to document it. I was now ready to learn the truth.

A few weeks later the phone rang, and Tyler answered it. He sounded confused talking to the person on the other line. He asked if they wanted to talk to Laural Wauters. After he hung up, he told me that there was a strange old woman who asked if this was our phone number, but then she was gone. He said an operator came on the phone and tried to reconnect the call, but it was disconnected. My heart jumped! I knew this was the same woman who had called on my birthday five years earlier.

I had to do something; this was the sign I had been waiting for.

I ran upstairs to grab the manila envelope I had been holding onto for the past 19 years. I opened it and searched for all the names and addresses I could read. I called the long-distance operator and asked for directory assistance in Frankfurt, Germany. I gave the operator my mother's name…nothing. The doctor's name…nothing, no listings. Then I asked for a woman named Henrietta, whom I assumed was the midwife. Yes! The operator found her name and gave me her telephone number. Now what? I didn't know how to speak German. If I called Henrietta, I wouldn't know how to talk to her. I needed someone who could talk for me. It was frustrating to not know how to speak German.

A friend at work suggested a friend of hers who was German. I went to his house the very next evening. Michael was a German engineer who had been working in the U.S. for the past year. I shared with him that I was adopted and trying to find my birth mother. I gave him my adoptions papers and explained how I had cross-referenced every name on them with a telephone operator in Frankfurt, Germany. The only name that matched was Henrietta's so I gave him her phone number to call. As he read my adoption papers, he said that Henrietta was actually the woman who had turned my mother into the police the day after I was born. Michael shook his head in disbelief, as he told me that she was the person responsible for my mother being put in jail, as well as setting up the adoption. I wondered who she was and why she had my birth mother arrested in the first place. I had always sensed Henrietta as the midwife who had delivered me, so this news was all very alarming. But I was hopeful that she would know something about who my birth mother was. Michael assured me that he would call Henrietta first thing in the morning. It was too late to call now for it was after midnight in Frankfurt.

CHAPTER 8: THE SECRET

I arrived at work the next morning to a message from Michael. He had called Henrietta and he wanted me to call him right back. I called him immediately.

He said, "Laural, you'd better sit down." I sat down at my desk, and then he proceeded to explain that he had just talked to Henrietta and that she was my grandmother!

I freaked out.

"What did you say?" I asked, although I knew perfectly well what he had said.

He said, "I asked her if she knew your mother, Karin, and she said, 'Yes, she is my daughter."

"I told her I was looking for her on behalf of Karin's daughter, Carmen Sylvia, who had been born on December 3, 1954. Your grandmother got very excited at the news and said her heart was beating 280 beats a minute."

My grandmother, Henrietta had given him my mother's telephone number. She went on to say that my mother was now living in Columbus, Georgia. He told me that Henrietta said she couldn't talk to him on the phone anymore because people were there, and she didn't want them to hear her. He said she thanked him and hung up.

I asked him if there was anything more he could tell me. "No," he said, other than that she seemed very nice and was really excited that I had found her.

The conversation had been very short; it seemed she couldn't speak freely and I found that curious. I was so thankful that Henrietta had given him my mother's phone number in that brief period of time. I couldn't help wonder why she felt she couldn't talk freely. Even more secrets?

After we ended our call, I started crying at my desk. Everyone from work began wondering what was going on with me. I quickly explained what had happened and prepared myself to go home and call my mother. I called Paul and told him to meet me at home immediately.

Driving home, I could barely keep it together.

I was intensely emotional: scared, excited, happy, and thrilled. My stomach was in knots; my heart was beating quickly. I must have been driving about 75 mph on our two-lane, country road. I cried and screamed during every mile of my 18-mile journey. Paul was already at home by the time I arrived!

I gave him a quick update and grabbed the phone with my heart pounding. When I called the phone number, a man answered. Flustered, I asked if Karin was there.

"No," he said.

"When will she be home?" I asked.

"Around 5," he replied.

Paul and I sat in our living room, numb with anticipation. I was watching the clock with nerves so tense I felt like I could spring wide open. I called again at 5:05. The man answered again, and when I asked if Karin was there, he again said "no."

"When will she be home?" I anxiously asked, probably sounding somewhat desperate.

"Later," he responded, and then he said rather impatiently, "Just give me your message, and I'll tell Karin."

I was really nervous about leaving a message with him; I didn't know if this was her husband and I might be dropping a bombshell, or even more improbably whether he might even be my father.

"Please tell her my name is Laural, and here is my telephone number, and that I think I am her daughter."

"Say what?" The man answered.

"I was born in Germany, and I have been looking for my birth mother. If she would like to talk to me, I would appreciate it," I continued.

He said, "Okay." And we hung up.

I started hyperventilating. I was so scared that I had just ruined everything by blabbing that information out on the phone to a perfect stranger.

Less than five minutes later, I had to call again back to clarify. "Hi, this is Laural. I don't know if I just made a big mistake telling you what I just told you. Please don't tell anyone but Karin."

He said he would keep it a secret. I asked if he knew anything about this. He said, "Yes."

"So, this isn't a shock to you?" I asked.

"No, but I can't guarantee how she is going to react." After these words, I said, "Thank you," and hung up.

I waited anxiously.

Nearly an hour later, the phone rang.

A beautiful, clear voice with a wonderful German accent asked me, "Is this Laural?"

"Yes," and I asked, "Is this Karin?"

"Yes," and then she cried out to me, "Please, please say something to me that lets me know it's really you!"

My mind was racing as I told her, "I was born in Frankfurt, Germany, on December 3, 1954, and my mother was Karin, and she named me Carmen Sylvia."

I started crying as she started crying.

"It's really you," she cried.

She went on, "There hasn't been a minute that has gone by that I haven't thought of you. I have loved you all of my life and have been praying that you would find me." Then she stopped and caught her breath.

"Laural, are you psychic?" she asked.

I hesitated for a moment before replying, "Yes."

She was actually relieved by my answer.

It confirmed what she had always felt, that I had inherited the family "gift." Karin told me that my great-grandmother was a psychic and neighborhood healer in Germany. She went on to explain how people came to her for help and advice. She had always hoped that one of her children would have the gift. Karin shared with me that she had the gift too, and it was through that gift that she knew that one day I would find her.

She stopped and said, "Laural, there is something you need to know before I go any further. You have two sisters and a brother and when I say that, I mean two full-blooded sisters and a brother. I am also their mother, and your father is also their father."

"How can that be?" I asked. My mind began racing as I started imagining the family that I never knew existed. How was I separated from a mother who wanted me?

Karin explained that I was stolen from her when she was put in jail for no reason. I asked her why she was in jail, but she didn't want to talk about it. She said her memory was weak, but at some point, my father came back into her life and they were married. I was shocked! Then I remembered my vision in college of her escaping from jail and realized it was a premonition of this truth. I also thought of my grandmother and wondered immediately if Karin knew what Henrietta had done. I felt I was on very slippery ground, and became mindful of how I worded my answers. I did not want to ruin this amazing moment.

Karin then said that she and my father had a child together before me, and they had named her Viola.

"Wait!" I said. "You mean I have an older sister?"

She said, "Yes, plus we had two other children after we got married. A son, Lonnie and a daughter Caroline."

In a voice that trembled, I asked if my father was still alive; had the man who answered the phone been him?

She told me that my father had died in 1976 of a heart attack. He had been in the Army his entire adult life and had just retired. She told me that they met when he was stationed in Frankfurt after World War II. He was eleven years older than she was, had fought in WWII, Korea and Vietnam, and he spoke seven languages.

"Who is the man that answered the phone?" I asked.

"He is an old friend of mine who lives with me to keep me company. Tell me, how did you find me?"

I could feel my hands sweat as I answered her question, "I received two very strange phone calls from an elderly German woman soon after my adoptive mother died. Both times she called and said that she had the wrong number and hung up." Karin sounded confused, which confirmed for me that she had not made the phone calls. But if not her, then who? And why did she not know about them?

"After the second phone call I pulled out my adoption papers and called the Frankfurt operator who was very patient with me as I read off names to see if they were listed in the phone directory. The only number that I was able to find was your mother Henrietta," I said.

"Why would Henrietta's name be on those papers?" she asked. Nervously I replied, "I'm not really sure, but I could mail you a copy of the papers and you could read them."

"Yes, please mail them to me right away. I want to see them for myself. Please tell me more of how you found me," she pleaded.

"After I had Henrietta's phone number, I found a friend who could speak German and I asked him to call her and see if she knew anything about you or me. When he called the number, Henrietta answered the phone.

He asked her if she knew either you or me, and that's when Henrietta said yes. She told him she was my grandmother. She immediately gave him your phone number and said that I should call you, her daughter, right away because you would want to know me. She told my friend that you had gotten married and that you now lived in Georgia. My friend told me that Henrietta was extremely excited and said her heart was beating 280 beats a minute," I said.

My mother was clearly upset by this news.

"Laural, this is too much for me to think about right now. It's too upsetting for me. Please, I just want to know who you are and listen to your voice," she said.

I told her that I loved trees and had large gardens filled with herbs and perennials; that I loved art and my favorite color was black and my favorite musician was John Lennon. She was excited because she was also passionate about art, gardening and music. When she told me that her favorite color was black and that she loved John Lennon I gasped in delight. She went on to explain how she owns an art and antique business. I could tell she was a soulful eccentric woman with an open mind and heart. I sensed that we were very much alike and she expressed that too!

"Your older sister, Viola, has been wanting to find you and know you, I can't wait any longer – I need to call her and let her know that I am actually talking with you right now." Karin promised that she would call me right back and then she ended our conversation by saying, "I love you."

This took my breath away. Gertrude had never told me she loved me, and now I was hearing these words I so longed for from a mother I had only dreamed of.

When I got off the phone, I was overwhelmed and in a state of shock. But before I could think too much, the phone rang. This time it was my sister Viola.

She started out by asking for Laural.

"Yes, this is me," I said.

She began crying, "This is your sister, Viola."

I had never even thought of having a sister – and here she was. We talked for two hours about everything. At one point, she said very matter-of-factly, "Well, you know, Mom is Jewish."

My heart jumped because I always felt that my mother could be Jewish, so I asked, "How could that be?"

Viola explained that our mother had learned, after the war was over, that her biological father was Jewish. She said he left her and Henrietta when Karin was only four years old to protect them from the Nazis. Viola told me that our mother began practicing Judaism privately, and when she came to the United States, she was excited to finally be able to go to a synagogue in Columbus, Georgia. However, the synagogue couldn't accept her as Jewish because her mother wasn't Jewish. Having a Jewish father was not enough. Karin was told she would have to go through a conversion process to be recognized in the Jewish faith. Viola told me that our mother was so upset by what happened that she never went into a synagogue again.

We talked about how terrified she must have felt living through the fear and confusion of growing up in Nazi Germany only to discover that her father, whom she never knew, was Jewish. And to then be denied her father's lineage, here in America. How heartbreaking.

I asked Viola about our father Lonnie. She told me he was a combination of Cherokee Indian and Scots Irish. What a combination. Now my ancestry was Jewish, German, Native American and Scots Irish? The collective wounds of victim and perpetrator stared me in the face. I tried to take this all in. I had been seeking a way to blend all that I learned about Native American and Celtic beliefs with world religions and indigenous cultures.

It was exciting to feel that I might actually be a meld of what I had been drawn to.

Viola told me that our mother broke down the day after our father's funeral and that's when she told Viola that she had a sister who was taken away at birth. From that day on, Viola said, she never stopped thinking about me. I began shaking, feeling the effects of the day, and asked if we could stop talking for now. She understood. I got her phone number and address, and she took mine. I promised I would send her a photo right away.

Later that night, I called Karin again.

I needed to know if all of this was real. She reassured me that it was. It was hard to believe I had found her and that I was loved. Then the conversation shifted abruptly.

"I have never forgiven my mother for not helping me, and now I learn that her name is on the adoption papers and she was involved in it all along. How could she do this to me?" asked Karin.

I pleaded, "Please try to forgive her and make peace with her. I think your mother Henrietta is also the one who brought us back together. I believe that she is the one who made the two mysterious phone calls that caused me to read my adoption papers and begin looking for you. She is now very old, and she must be feeling guilty for what she did and maybe she is trying to fix it."

Karin went silent as she reflected on what I said. We were both clearly conflicted having to deal with such an intense sense of betrayal and also the joy of finally being reunited at the same time. Suddenly my mother responded, "Maybe both of those calls happened when Henrietta unexpectedly showed up here, at the airport in Columbus. During both visits she asked if I wanted to find you. I asked her why she was bringing up something that hurt so badly and taunting me with something that was impossible."

I sensed my mother was beginning to accept that Henrietta had been trying to repair her role in my adoption.

She asked again for me to send her the adoption papers and some photos of myself. We said good night.

"I love you Laural," were her last words to me that night. I went to bed with a heart full of questions. It seemed that for each answer I received, there was another question. My mother was insistent on not telling me certain things over the phone, but what I did know was that I was loved and that my birth mother was not a "no good drunken prostitute" or a "bad seed." I went to sleep with a new dream to dream.

The next day, my other sister Caroline called me; or, I should say, her husband Brad, called. He called to break the ice, and then Caroline got on the phone. She sounded a little apprehensive and I sensed she was feeling some pressure to feel instantly like sisters.

I assured Caroline, "I could never be what Viola is to you. We didn't share 30 years of growing up together like you and Viola. I never dreamt of having two sisters and a brother, so I feel as surprised about this as you do. But now that we are aware of each other, we can develop a relationship that is unique to us." Caroline seemed to feel more comfortable.

A few days later, my mother called to tell me that she had received the photos and the adoption papers I sent. She said I looked like her, my father, and my three siblings all rolled into one.

She also told me how she had called Henrietta to let her know that we had reunited on the phone. Karin said she thanked Henrietta for giving my friend her telephone number but was shocked when my grandmother denied everything! She denied talking with my friend, giving anyone my mother's phone number or knowing anything about me. I was totally confused, and so was Karin.

It didn't make any sense. I then recalled how my friend Michael said that Henrietta couldn't talk freely and hung up very quickly. I wondered if it was all related. I shared this with Karin and asked why Henrietta would do this. Karin became quiet, as silent tension filled miles of space between us, until she said, "I can't tell you the full story of what happened and how I lost you unless you are here in person."

"I'll come as soon as Paul and I can both get off of work and after Tyler is done with school," I replied.

This was all so confusing and of course I wanted to know as much as possible. I made arrangements for Paul, Tyler, and myself to drive down to Georgia that summer.

We left in June and drove all the way to Nashville the first night. We arrived in Columbus around 5 p.m. the following day. When we walked into our hotel room there was a beautiful blue vase filled with wildflowers sitting on a table near the window. I read the card; it was from my Karin. This was the first time I had ever received flowers from a mother. This was foreign to me, but it felt so good.

Karin's words on the card were, "I love you and I can't wait any longer to see you. Call me as soon as you read this." I started crying and called her right away.

She answered impatiently, "Where are you?"

I said we were at the hotel and she responded, "We'll be right over."

Paul, Tyler, and I went down to the lobby to get a Coke. In that exact moment Viola and Karin walked into the lobby. We recognized each other immediately from the photos we had sent each other. We hugged and cried and found a place in the lobby to just sit and look at each other in giddy disbelief.

Eventually we drove to my mother's home on Peacock Street. It was enchanting! There was a huge magnolia tree in front with two palm trees on each side of the driveway. The front porch featured white pillars standing in front of a red brick exterior. Large green ferns hung from the porch and two cement lions guarded the door. A massive wood door opened directly into the stunning living area. Inside were deep red walls, black and white floor tiles, plus lots of art and tapestry rugs.

A large portrait of my father, Lonnie, hung in the living room facing the front door. I was mesmerized as I looked into his eyes. He had a penetrating yet approachable gaze. He was in uniform and very handsome. I could see his Cherokee heritage in his cheekbones, something I could now see that I inherited from him.

My biological father Lonnie.

My mother had painted all the walls in her house white with bold, black geometric borders. Her creative spirit was everywhere. I sensed it was something we shared.

She wanted to talk to me privately in her backyard. When she opened the back door, I stepped into a magical garden filled with curving beds of hostas and perennials that were freshly edged and mulched. As we walked under an immense old tree, Karin began to express her anger toward my parents for taking me away from her.

"What do you mean?" I asked.

"They stole you from me and I can't forgive them for doing that," she stated very matter-of-factly.

I could see both the anger and the sadness in her face and she could see the shock and confusion in mine.

I had no clue what she was talking about. Then she shook her head, as if trying to release that thought from her mind. "Tell me, how did they treat you?" she asked.

In that moment my whole life flashed before my eyes. I couldn't tell her the truth for I didn't know the truth anymore. I carefully explained that my parents were both good people who had given me everything I needed, including a college education. I knew that if I told Karin about the abuse Gertrude inflicted on me it would upset her and I didn't want to give her any more reasons to be angry. I had worked so hard to heal my relationship with Gertrude and I was still missing her. I did tell Karin that I had brought a VHS tape of home movies from when I lived in Germany, if she wanted to see me as a child. She said she wasn't sure she wanted to see it yet, because she was still too angry.

I shared that my father was a quiet man with a good sense of humor. He was gentle, strong and wise...

She abruptly stopped me, "I heard he was a general."

Surprised, I replied, "No, but he was with the CIA."

She retorted, "Henrietta told me you were adopted by very important people and that your father was a general for the United States Army."

Looking intensely for my reaction, I shook my head "no" because from what I knew my father wasn't a general. I wondered why Henrietta would say that.

Karin wrapped her arms around me, pulling me gently to her heart, as if her soul finally realized who I was. "I'm so sad that I missed watching you grow up. Just think how much fun we would have had tending to this garden and talking about life. We are so much alike."

I began realizing that this meeting was far more intense for her than it was for me. I was the daughter she had loved and longed for, ever since I had been taken from her.

I was also learning that I had a mother who loved me.

We slowly walked around to the front of the house soaking in the sweetness of our mutual awareness. Her front porch greeted us as one of the ferns brushed my face. I could feel a cool breeze coming from two ceiling fans under her white-washed porch. When we opened the front door, Tyler and Paul greeted us in the living room.

Karin adored them both, Tyler looked a lot like her, Paul remained quiet, taking it all in. We sat on the couch together when Karin asked if she could watch the home movies I had brought. I was both pleasantly surprised and extremely nervous. She invited Viola and her kids to join us as I fumbled around praying that the tape would play on her equipment. Once everything was working I sat down next to her and she held my hand as we watched.

Karin got excited when she recognized places that she knew. Tears of gratitude began to flow as she saw how loving my parents were to me and how well dressed and happy I looked. Her anger seemed to dissipate as we were both very grateful to Gertrude for this gift. It was a long day.

I didn't sleep very well that night. I knew the upcoming day would be even more intense. Karin had promised to tell us "the story." I was also looking forward to meeting my brother, Lonnie and my sister Caroline.

When we knocked on the door that morning, my mother answered. She told me Lonnie and his wife, Julie, had arrived late the previous evening after working all day. They lived north of Atlanta and had just woken up. Lonnie was taking a shower when I arrived. I sat anxiously waiting for him, and then I heard him walk up behind me. I got up, turned around, and hugged him. When I pulled back, our eyes met for the first time. It was intense. I could see right inside of him. He had my eyes, and it was like looking at myself. I instantly loved him. Lonnie and I didn't talk much; we didn't have to. We just sat there and stared at each other.

Soon Viola came with her husband and three children; all that remained was Caroline who lived in Norfolk, Virginia with her husband Brad. He was stationed in the Air Force there. She had promised me on the phone that she, Brad, and the kids would come and that they would be here this morning too. But for some reason, she wanted to keep it a surprise. She had sworn me to secrecy and had told Karin they wouldn't be able to come. I kept stalling, trying to prevent everyone from getting into too heavy a conversation about anything until they arrived. It was hard, but it worked. Soon I heard their car. Nobody knew who it was until Caroline got out of her van. Why she chose to do this, I didn't know, but I played along. All that mattered was that we were all together! Our mother was beside herself. All four of her children were together, finally.

It was Father's Day weekend – June 19, 1994 – and it was very clear that Karin wanted to be with her four children to tell us what had really happened.

Paul took the hint and invited everyone to swim in the pool at our hotel. It was a great

Viola (left) Lonnie (top) Me (right) Caroline (bottom) Mom (center)

solution since there were six grandchildren and four adults.

After they left, Karin had the four of us sit on the couch in front of her. For the first time in her life, she was going to tell the story of how she grew up, how she met our father and how she lost me. I could sense that everyone was anxious and a little confused.

Karin said she was born on July 7, 1933 in Heddernheim outside Frankfurt, Germany. That year Adolph Hitler became the Chancellor of the Third Reich.

She grew up not knowing her father, Johannes, who fled the country in 1936 when she was only three years old. She was told, after the war, that the reason he left was because he was Jewish and that her mother, his wife, Henrietta had decided to join the Nazi party.

My heart skipped a few beats as I tried to comprehend what I had just heard. My grandmother Henrietta was a Nazi and she was married to a Jewish man?? How could that be? My mind was spinning as Karin spoke.

Karin explained that she lived with her maternal grandparents, Heinrich and Bertha. Karin was Henrietta's only child and Henrietta was the only child of Heinrich and Bertha so they welcomed their only grandchild into their life.

Heinrich owned and operated a corner grocery store in Heddernheim. They lived above the store, which had two apartments. Bertha also worked as a neighborhood psychic and healer. People would come to the store to buy groceries and many would also go upstairs to see my great-grandmother for help or guidance. I thought how odd it was that my mother lived above a grocery store just like I did and that my great grandmother was a healer.

In 1944, when the Allied Forces bombed Frankfurt, she and her grandparents moved to the countryside for safety.

They lived in tents outside the city. She went to school there as well. Heinrich was an outspoken opponent of the Nazi party, and several times the SS came to their house to question his loyalty.

Karin, is the one holding a book. (second from left) Taken at a tent school near the coal mines outside Heddernheim in 1944.

She described how she once saw an officer pin her grandfather up against the wall to intimidate him, but he held strong. A Jewish work camp was nearby. Soldiers marched prisoners, tied together with rope, past their store. Heinrich would secretly drop apples on the ground from his tree for the men to pick up and eat later.

Karin told us how her grandparents often expressed disbelief that their only child, Henrietta, chose to leave her daughter and join the Third Reich. The angst on our mother's face was palpable as she recalled the fact that Henrietta never visited her as she grew up during the war.

Karin didn't even know her father's last name and had no memory of him. She told us about a time when her grandparents encouraged her to visit her father's mother in Solingen. They pinned a little star onto her jacket and put her on a train all by herself. She remembered meeting her grandmother but not her grandfather. She recalled how beautiful she was. Karin described her as having very dark hair and dark piercing eyes. She couldn't recall much else.

"Why did Bertha and Heinrich do this?" we asked.

"They wanted me to meet my other grandmother because it might be the only chance I would ever get to see her," she said.

I thought how risky this was yet how brave my mother had been. What a gift she had received to meet her Jewish grandmother. I was so proud of her and of my great grandparents for helping her make this happen. We asked Karin if she ever heard from her again. She lowered her eyes and said no. She felt she had perished in the Holocaust.

Karin continued telling us how they returned to Heddernheim in 1945, after the war was over. The grocery store had been looted and the windows were broken.

Two years later, when Karin was fourteen, Henrietta appeared in her bedroom in the middle of the night.

Karin didn't know who she was and began screaming. Henrietta tried to calm her down by explaining that she was her mother and had come home to live. The next morning Karin learned that she also had a half-brother. Henrietta introduced Hans as the son of her late husband, a German soldier, who was killed in Russia during the war. Henrietta and Hans had been living in Bavaria and shared a home with a close friend or relative of Heinrich Himmler, who visited often.

What?!? My minded raced...Himmler was one of the most powerful people within the Nazi party. He led the SS and Gestapo. He oversaw the construction of concentration camps. Himmler was actually the person most directly responsible for the Holocaust! I felt an energetic knife pierce my heart as I realized how close my grandmother was to one of the evilest people to ever live on this Earth.

Karin went on to tell us how Henrietta often boasted that she had daily access to Hitler's personal retreat, the Eagle's Nest, as well as top-secret clearance to an underground command center. She also worked at Bergen-Belsen for a short time when it was a holding camp.

As I heard these words, I remembered that this was the concentration camp Anne Frank had died in! I was horrified as Karin shared these stories. I feared that my worst nightmare was coming true. I was now realizing that I may be ancestrally related to a Nazi. My palms started to sweat, but I didn't say anything because I didn't want to upset anyone. They all seemed so very calm about this, so I just tried to breathe through it.

Karin explained that when the war ended in 1945, Henrietta was captured and accused of being a war criminal. Henrietta spent two years in an internment camp in France. Upon her release in 1947, Henrietta returned to Frankfurt. She and Hans moved into the apartment below them.

Karin shared how her friends were young, free thinkers who had opposed the Nazi regime. They were "German beatniks" – artists, poets, actors, and philosophers. Several of her friends were also gay. During the war, the Nazi Party would have had them killed. Karin explained how she hated and feared her mother Henrietta and was disgusted by her stories of being a Nazi. She was so ashamed. None of her friends knew anything about who her mother was.

Karin was working at a daycare center, when she noticed a handsome older man teaching a class in the same building. She was 16 at the time. Two years later he walked into her favorite coffeehouse and noticed her watching him, so he came over and introduced himself. Karin described our father as an intelligent, gentle and attractive man. There was an instant connection, and during the following two weeks he came to the coffeehouse every day to see her. They entered into a relationship that became passionate and intense. Karin was now 18 and it was the early 1950s. Life was difficult in post-war Germany. Frankfurt had been destroyed by bombs and struggled to rebuild. Money and all that came with it was in short supply. Many of Frankfurt's young men had lost their lives during the war, and American servicemen now occupied the city. Birth control was not available and young German women often found themselves pregnant by American soldiers. This was a very precarious situation, as American GIs were prohibited from having relationships with German women. If they fathered a child, they could be discharged from duty and the mother could lose custody. These children often became outcasts by their family and were placed in orphanages as "war children."

Early into their relationship, Karin discovered she was pregnant. When Karin gave Lonnie the news, he immediately distanced himself from her. Lonnie explained that it was dangerous for them to be seen together anymore.

This news both shocked and confused Karin as it broke her heart. Lonnie tried to reassure her that he loved her very much and promised to send money via friends to support her and the baby. He also asked Karin to not speak of him or try to find him. Plus, she shouldn't tell anyone that he was the father. In a matter of moments, Lonnie left. Karin stood in the coffeehouse pregnant, alone and heartbroken.

She told us how she moved on with her life and how she gave birth to a healthy baby girl in a small neighborhood hospital. Karin brought her baby home to her grandparents. But life was tense and uneasy as she tried to come to grips with being an unwed mother with a secret American lover. One day she got word that Lonnie wanted to see his baby girl and how he wanted to name her Viola. Then, just as suddenly as he appeared, he disappeared.

I could see Viola getting both sentimental and agitated as she listened intently to our mother's every word.

Our mother told us how she was furious with Lonnie for leaving again and out of desperation and anger she decided to marry Dietrich, a dear friend of hers who was also a gay dentist. The marriage was one of convenience. She was an unwed mother in need of a husband, and he was a single gay man who needed a cover. Karin left her grandparent's apartment to start a new life with Dietrich and Viola.

A few months later, Lonnie came to the coffeehouse looking for Karin. He had heard that she had married another man, and wanted to know if she still loved him. When he found her, Karin said she didn't want to talk to him; she fled away in a taxi. Lonnie jumped into another taxi and followed her. Finally, Karin stopped and they agreed to go to a hotel where they could talk in private. Here, Lonnie professed his love and tried to help Karin understand why he could not marry her. He told Karin that he was an Army sharpshooter who had to go on special assignments around the world.

He explained that his job was extremely demanding and highly sensitive. He said it would be dangerous for both Karin and Viola to be associated with him. He told Karin that he was originally sent to protect Karin because her mother was a Nazi and both the CIA and the KGB were watching her. Even though Karin was confused by it all, she said she understood. Then silence surrounded us as Karin told us that they spent that night in the hotel, which was the night she got pregnant with me. Lonnie left the next morning.

Karin said she was relieved to know the reasons why Lonnie couldn't be with her and that she understood why she had to keep their relationship a secret. She told us how she knew with all her heart that Lonnie did truly love her. A month later she was shocked and frightened when she discovered that she was pregnant again.

What a bizarre situation this was for my mother and now for me. Karin smiled at me knowingly. With a heavy sigh she explained how she told Dietrich she was pregnant. He was angry and filed for an immediate annulment of their marriage. He didn't want to be responsible for me and feared what people would think. They went to court where a judge determined that Dietrich was eligible for an annulment by citing that his wife had an extramarital affair.

I thought this must be why my mother Gertrude said Karin was a "whore." I also reflected on my adoption papers and seeing Dietrich's name as my mother's husband. This was all so fascinating and yet so frightening at the same time. But I was grateful to finally be learning the truth.

Karin became a little sentimental as she wistfully recalled her friendship with Dietrich, "Dear poor Dietrich, I put him through so much during all of this. His poor nerves, I wonder what happened to him."

After Karin allowed her heart to settle back into the moment, she explained what happened next.

She and Viola, who was now a one-year-old, returned back to her grandparents' apartment. Henrietta lived in the apartment below, but Karin still wanted nothing to do with her. She told us that when she went into labor, Henrietta insisted on taking her to the hospital and being with her in the delivery room. Karin refused, but Henrietta wouldn't take "no" for an answer. She hated her mother for being a Nazi and she didn't want Henrietta's face to be the first face her baby would see.

I felt myself squirming inside, feeling the tension that surrounded my birth. Everyone else looked enthralled.

Karin told us how she began pleading to the nurses that she didn't want her baby to come out in her mother's presence. No one listened to her so she tried to hold me in. They sat her on a bucket and asked Henrietta to hold her down to induce contractions until I came out. I was born over a bucket on December 3, 1954.

I had sensed Henrietta had been my mother's midwife. Now I understood why.

Karin named me Carmen Sylvia, not thinking of what my father might have wanted. I asked her why. She said it sounded artistic and dramatic. At the hospital she nursed me and loved me. When she was released, she brought me to her grandparents' where Viola was waiting.

Then the mood changed abruptly as Karin became very agitated. She recalled how she was stopped on the stairs by Henrietta who started shouting at her, "Get out, get out and take that bastard child with you!" Our great-grandmother opened the door at the top of the staircase holding Viola in her arms. Karin told us how Henrietta turned around and pointed her finger at her own mother and told her to stay quiet. Henrietta then pointed her finger at Karin and ordered her to leave the building. She said that we were not welcome there anymore.

Confused and scared, with nowhere to go, Karin brought me back to the hospital. Apparently, in the few minutes it had taken, my name was still on the hospital crib. Karin then explained how they took me back but not her. They did ask Karin to come every day to nurse me and to bring extra milk with her. With nowhere to go, she crashed with some of her friends.

For the next few days, she came to the hospital to nurse me, hold me and love me. Then one day I was gone. She panicked and immediately questioned where I was, but instead of answers the police arrested her for vagrancy. She tried to explain that she was not a vagrant. They put her in jail and said that she was not fit to be a mother.

Karin was now crying recalling how confused she was and that she couldn't understand why she was put in jail. The police called her a vagrant and she was unfit because she didn't have a husband. She couldn't tell anyone who my real father was, for it would put everyone in danger. The next day the adoption agency began pushing her to sign the papers that would relinquish her rights as my mother. She pleaded with them to let her see me and asked that they take good care of me until she got out of jail. They refused to let her see me and said that she had no rights.

We could all see how hard this was on our mother as she shared this part of the story. She sat down in exhaustion, as she said that everything became a blur while she was in jail. She told us that she had become suicidal and despondent when she realized that she would not be released unless she agreed to give me up for adoption.

Eleven long months went by until one day a "big fat lawyer" came and pressured her into signing an unconditional release that gave away her rights as my mother. This meant that I could be legally adopted. He told her that this was the only way she would ever get out of jail.

By this point, Karin said she felt she had no choice; she signed the papers and walked out of jail in a daze. She told us that her only bright spot was knowing that she would see Viola again, who was now two years old. Viola had been living with her great-grandparents all this time.

Viola, Caroline and my brother Lonnie were now visibly shocked. With jaws dropped, we all tried to comprehend what we just heard. The energy and heat in the room became noticeably intense.

"Mom, why didn't Dad rescue you from jail?" Lonnie asked.

She replied, "He was away on assignment, and had no way to contact me. But your father showed up within days of my release and immediately moved Viola and me to a house in Bad Kreuznach. He paid for all of our expenses. I was more upset with your grandmother Henrietta and why *she* didn't help me get out of jail."

Karin said that after she was released Henrietta told her that an important American general had adopted me, and the US government had taken control, so she couldn't help.

I started wondering what my adoptive parents' roles were in this tragic mess. Did they know that my mother Karin had wanted desperately to keep me? Or did they actually play a part in taking me against her will? Either way, I now understood why Karin was so upset with them when we talked in her yard the day before. She had every right to feel that Gertrude and John were responsible for taking me from her against her will.

Karin had always believed that Henrietta was helpless. But now, after reading my adoption papers, she realized that Henrietta had actually been the one who turned her into the police, which opened the door for my adoption. Betrayal and confusion filled the air as we sat there trying to comprehend the enormity of what this meant to each of us.

I spoke up first by sharing that my adoptive father had been the chief of a CIA Unit in Frankfurt. I explained, "My father's job was to spy on spies and recruit ex-Nazis or German nationals to become agents for the United States to spy on the KGB and other spies." I went on to say, "I am beginning to think that maybe our grandmother Henrietta may have been an agent who worked for my father or knew one of his agents." No one responded.

I thought it to be entirely possible that she was thinking this could ultimately help our mother, herself, and me along with a childless couple. I began to suspect that Henrietta may not be the villain my mother Karin thought she was. I saw her as a tragic figure that was now feeling the guilt of what she had done. I was convinced that she was the one who had called me. It all began to make sense to me. If she had been an agent for my father John, or a friend of one of his agents, she would have been able to find me because she knew my name and who my adoptive parents were. What I couldn't reconcile was why our grandmother would join the Nazi party to begin with. My mind wondered if she had been a double agent all along and knowingly infiltrated the Nazi elite to gather information. If that were true this would be really crazy.

After a few moments of silent reflection, Karin continued to tell us that she and Viola lived in the house Lonnie had provided for them and how our father was able to freely visit whenever he could. When he did, they lived together as if they were married. Viola began to share happy memories of being with our father and how thoughtful and affectionate he was. Karin told us that in 1961 Lonnie chose to officially claim Viola as his daughter so she could have his last name. She also explained that Lonnie received a letter requesting his presence by the US Provost Marshall to discuss the possibility that I may be his daughter as well.

Karin was so hopeful at the very thought that I might be returned to her. She waited with great anticipation for the news she so desperately wanted to hear.

When Lonnie returned, he told Karin that he was directed by the US Provost Marshall's office to sign a form that relinquished his rights as my father. He then became very serious and stern as he forced her to take an oath of secrecy to never talk about me again. From that day on she was forbidden to say my name or acknowledge that I ever existed. I had to be completely dead to both of them; for her sake and for mine. She had to let me go once and for all. Karin was so scared and stunned by his directness and intensity that she agreed with him outwardly, but secretly and inwardly, she knew she could never let me go.

She said, "I always believed deep down that if I kept you alive in my heart that you would find me and you did."

My heart started racing at the thought of what this meant. I was immediately reminded that 1961 was the exact year when we suddenly left Germany. I remembered my adoptive father John telling me how we left because his cover was blown. As I began piecing this together in my mind, I realized that this was all probably related. I imagined my father John and my father Lonnie realizing for the first time who they each were to me and to each other. I wondered if they knew each other personally. They both had to know the circumstances that my mother had endured and the ramifications that my adoption now presented. I wondered what role Henrietta played in this drama and if Lonnie knew that Henrietta was responsible for setting this up to begin with. What agreement had my father Lonnie and John made? I remained silent, but my mind was in overdrive.

Karin continued to explain how she and Lonnie were married in 1963, and how they had two more children, Lonnie Jr. and Caroline.

In 1972, they moved to the United States and settled in Columbus, Georgia. Lonnie began his military career at Fort Benning in 1939, before Pearl Harbor and WWII.

Karin explained that in 1973, our father retired from the Army. He served his country in active duty during WWII, the Korean War, the Cold War and Vietnam. Plus, he went on special assignments for long periods of time. Viola shared a time when she remembered seeing our father's face in a *Life* magazine article; the story was about Argentina and Lonnie was in the background. My mind flashed on stories about Argentina and how prominent Nazis had fled there after the war, including Adolph Eichmann, Klaus Barbie and Josef Mengele. I also knew that Argentina played a pivotal role during the Cuban Missile Crisis. I felt like I was in the middle of a suspenseful spy novel.

In 1976, my brother Lonnie found him lying dead in the driveway. Lonnie, Viola, and Caroline immediately began sharing memories of our father.

"I remember sitting on the kitchen counter one night talking with Dad, when all of a sudden he grabbed me and we hit the floor. A bullet came shooting through the kitchen window and it was aimed right at us! Dad saved my life that night," said Caroline.

"I remember when some 'guys' in a big black car came to the house and pressured Mom to give them $50,000 from our father's pension, leaving us broke," said Lonnie.

"I remember how Dad would secretly make small fires in the backyard and burn little black books," said Viola.

"Mom, why didn't you call the police and order an autopsy on Dad after he died?" asked Lonnie.

Karin became very upset and said it was too complicated to explain and that she didn't want to talk about that. Lonnie then painfully recalled his experience of finding our father slumped over the open trunk of their car.

He said that our father had strange spots all over his body. He felt our father had been murdered somehow, and began questioning Mom as to why she didn't call the police. She kept telling him that he didn't understand how dangerous the whole thing was for all of them. Obviously, our father's death and what had happened was still very raw.

Karin pulled herself together, determined to get through everything that she wanted us to know. She went on to tell us about our father's death pact with her based on the secret and classified nature of his work. She said that he could never be given any form of anesthesia which could inadvertently cause him to talk about what it was that he knew or did. She told us that if he ever needed any kind of surgery, she would have to let him die. She said he kept cyanide pills in the heel of his shoe that could be used to kill him instantly. I thought to myself: what exactly did he do or know that he would be willing to kill himself for it?

At this point Caroline and Viola began to speak up on how they had always felt that Dad was a "hit man," but they had never really talked about it until now. They told me how he always had a small pistol tucked in the back of his pants, even at home. Karin confirmed that he even slept with it. My sisters continued to talk and told me that our father began doing side jobs for the CIA and Mafia after his retirement. I sensed Karin was relieved that they knew this so she didn't have to explain it any further.

My mind flashed to stories I had heard of the CIA and the Mafia working together. I then remembered the tiny little handgun I found in my father John's closet. I imagined Lonnie's gun looked like his. It was four or five inches long.

Lonnie brought up the day after our father's funeral when some men in a big black car came to the house and took Karin away. Karin said they forced her to sign release papers that stripped them of our father's military pension.

My brother Lonnie was visibly upset as to why she let them do this. "I had no choice and I can't talk about it. What is done is done. From that point on I had to figure out a way to provide for all of you by myself," Karin said.

Karin suddenly got up and left the room. We sat quietly on the oversized couch in her living room. Then all of a sudden, she walked back in with an armful of extension phones. She handed one to each of us. She said that she wanted me to hear my grandmother Henrietta's voice so I could confirm if she was indeed the same person who had called me at my home. Karin also wanted to know if Henrietta was the person who my friend Michael had talked with. Karin was confused and upset by Henrietta's denial of everything and needed to understand what had happened and why. This was her mother and she wanted answers.

She asked us all to go to separate rooms in the house and plug our phones in the outlets to form a big party line. I heard Karin dial the number as I nervously waited in the back bedroom. Henrietta answered the phone in German. Her voice sounded different; as if she had just woken up. In the beginning Henrietta was talking very quietly but as Karin asked questions, Henrietta's voice became more agitated.

Karin and Viola were speaking German and trying to explain that I was on the phone with them in Columbus so we could talk to each other. I couldn't understand a word they said except for my name. The conversation ended abruptly, when Henrietta hung up on all of us.

After we each put down our phones, we gathered in the living room. Viola and Karin tried to explain what had just happened. Henrietta apparently told them that she was worried that our conversation was being tapped; that she was being interrogated; and that she may have to commit suicide or be killed. Karin and Viola both said they were very confused and agreed that Henrietta must be getting senile.

I could see the hurt in my mother's eyes, as I knew she was hoping for some answers regarding Henrietta and my adoption. I understood that hurt all too well.

Even though I couldn't understand what Henrietta was saying, she didn't sound senile. Her voice was different than the one I had heard five years ago, but she had spoken to me in English and talked very softly. Now she was speaking German and was clearly agitated. We didn't get the answers or clarity we had hoped for, just more questions.

Karin changed the subject by telling us how she started her own business after our father died. She began a resale business by driving and picking up the good "junk" from people's garbage piles at night. Lonnie rode with her, and would jump out of the car to retrieve objects she spotted. Gradually she built up her clientele by selling her "finds" from the house. Once she had enough inventory, she opened her own shop named Pirouette. It was located in a historic building in downtown Columbus. She sold items on consignment, specializing in art and antiques. She was excited to show it to me, so we all decided to head downtown

to her shop. As I walked in the door I was amazed at what she had created. The store was in an old, renovated building. The space was long and narrow and had its original wood floors, brick walls, and pressed tin

Pirouette - Karin's store in Columbus, Georgia - 1994

ceiling. It was filled to the rafters with art, antiques and collectibles. I was mesmerized imagining myself sitting with her and spending time together talking for hours on end.

117

It was surprisingly similar in shape and architecture to our grocery store in Algoma. I wondered how strange it was that both of my mothers had operated their own retail businesses in charming old buildings.

When we returned to her house and I could see how Karin's ascetic for art and antiques filled her life. She had impeccable taste and an obvious love of ballet. Her style was very European: eclectic, sophisticated and natural. I wanted to soak it all in, when suddenly our precious window of time closed. Paul and Tyler, along with everyone else walked through the front door. The sacred space we were living in for the past eight hours was now replaced with a flurry of activity. It was getting late, and the kids needed to get ready for bed. Paul happily took Tyler back to the hotel.

Karin said she would bring me when I was ready to go. Viola decided to stay with us as well. Within an hour the house was empty. The three of us sat around the kitchen table. My heart was filled with questions and emotions. Karin could sense my frustration.

She comforted me by saying, "Don't worry, Laural. We will have many years together. I'm only 60 years old and I'm healthy,"

Then she looked straight at me and asked, "Laural, can you please call me Mom instead of Karin?"

My heart stopped. I was so not prepared for this question right now. I answered her without thinking it through by saying, "I'm sorry, but it's not easy for me to call you Mom because Gertrude was my mom. I still miss her very much. I'm overwhelmed by everything I've just learned. I know in time I'll be comfortable saying it but not right now. I hope you understand. It's complicated."

I could see that my response hurt Karin deeply as tears began streaming down her face. Then, all of a sudden, she stood up, grabbed her car keys and ran out of the house.

Viola and I sat there, numbed by what had just happened. As we heard our mother's car pull out of the driveway and down the darkened street I asked Viola, "Where do you think she is going?" Viola said she didn't know. We patiently waited for her to come back home.

I was so mad at myself and wished I could take it all back. The last thing I wanted to do was hurt this amazing woman who was my birth mother. She had already endured so much pain because of me and I did not want to create any more. As we waited, I reflected on everything she had told us and realized how brave she was and how much I loved and admired her.

Shortly after midnight we finally heard Karin drive into the driveway. When she walked into the kitchen, she was completely exhausted and looked as if she had been crying for hours. Viola and I were still sitting at the kitchen table, exactly where she left us.

She looked at me and said quietly, "Laural, please get ready and I'll drive you back to your hotel now. I know it's late and you need your rest."

When I walked outside, the warm still air of a hot Georgia night greeted me. It was filled with suspense as I silently slid into the passenger's seat of my mother's car. She drove me through the unfamiliar streets of Columbus and I wondered how many trips like this we had missed.

"I'm so sorry for hurting you," I said. "I never meant to do that. I'm just so confused by everything."

"It's okay, Laural. I know I have to be patient. I've waited this long; I can wait a little longer," she replied.

I could feel her wanting me to relax and enjoy the fact that we were finally alone and together. Just sitting next to each other riding in her car brought us both comfort.

"Can I ask you where you went?" I asked.

"I went to the cemetery to be with your father and talk to him about everything. I told him about you and that you were here in Columbus sitting in our kitchen. I also told him that I had finally shared our story with all four children. Being with him gives me comfort," she answered.

When we finally reached the hotel, she stopped the car and turned off the engine. Before she could say a word I immediately said, "I never want to lose you again." I reached over and hugged her from the depths of my heart, so she could feel how much I loved her. I held her like a child holds its mother, letting her know that I would always love her.

Karin began crying. "I don't want ever want to lose you again either, and this hug tells me everything I needed to know," she held my face in her hands and said, "I love you, Laural."

"I love you too," I said adamantly.

We could feel the energy begin to shift as we realized how relieved we both were. Then she chuckled. "Don't you think our life story could be a book or even a movie?"

"Oh, my God! Yes! This is crazy!" I laughed.

Then she gently held my hand to her heart. "Laural, please. I want the truth to be told about what happened to us, and you are the one to do it."

Then she smiled and said, "When the book becomes a movie, I want Olympia Dukakis to play me!"

What a fantastic dream that would be! I thought.

We hugged again as Karin whispered, "I will pick you up in the morning for Father's Day brunch, my treat."

That next morning our mother gathered us together like a mother hen gathering her chicks. The intensity of the day before was now replaced by pure joy as the story had been told and we were all still together. The special Father's Day brunch was being held in the same hotel we were in.

We greeted her in the lobby where our eyes first met a few days ago. She looked so proud to have us all with her. We were finally a family sitting around a very large table in a fancy dining room drinking mimosas, juice and coffee. The look on her face was priceless as she was clearly relieved to have released the secrets and stories she had held onto for so long. She looked magnificent dressed in black, wearing Egyptian revival earrings that draped to her shoulders. I was so proud to be her daughter.

Surrounded by my new extended family we raised our glasses to toast Lonnie, our father and grandfather.

Today was Father's Day. Even though he wasn't with us, we were all grateful to celebrate together for the first time as a family.

My mother Karin's smile was filled with endless possibilities as we began to plan for our new life together.

"Sometimes our fate resembles a fruit tree in winter.
Who would think that those branches would turn green
again and blossom, but we hope it, we know it."
- Johann Wolfgang von Goethe -

CHAPTER 9 – THE IMPOSSIBLE

On the way home, we took a different route through the Smoky Mountains in North Carolina. They were magical. At the entrance to the Smoky Mountain National Park is a town called Cherokee. There was a sign telling us that an educational center focused on the Cherokee people was just ahead. In that moment I realized that I was on the ancestral land of the Cherokee and had been feeling the pull of this land for the past fifty miles. I asked Paul to stop at the educational center. I was curious to see how I would feel walking among the artifacts. I wanted to feel connected to the Cherokee and possibly my father's lineage.

I could see a resemblance between myself, my father, and the photos and portraits of the Cherokee people on the walls. I bought several books for reference, hoping to trace my lineage more accurately. I also bought a dream catcher before we continued our drive to the top of one of the mountains. Once we arrived at the summit, we stopped and looked south over the Smoky Mountains. It was breathtaking and gave me a sense of feeling like I was home.

We had brought a video camera with us. Paul videotaped me waving good-bye to my birth family from the top of that mountain. When we got home, I took all of the video footage that I had shot and had it edited together with some music and words. I sent a copy to my mother and my three siblings as a remembrance of us all being together.

A week later, Tyler answered the phone. He said an elderly woman asked for me by name in a strange accent. When he told her that I wasn't home she gave him her phone number and asked him to have me call her back.

When Tyler handed me the number, I was shocked! It was Henrietta's number! It was the exact same number I had received from the phone operator in Frankfurt and the same number that I had given to my friend Michael to call. This was the number that Henrietta answered when he talked to her! This absolutely confirmed for me that she was indeed the person who had made the two mysterious phone calls.

I wondered how she had found me and how long she had kept my location a secret. She must have known my father John's name in order to have found me. I sensed that she had silently been watching me all of my life.

I wondered why she helped Michael, a total stranger, bring my mother and me together, and why she flatly denied any involvement when Karin asked her. Why was she so afraid when we were all on the phone together and why was she calling now? I sensed Henrietta may be in some sort of trouble just as she had told us on the phone in Georgia.

I immediately called Karin and asked if she had heard from Henrietta. She said, "Yes, shortly after you left Georgia. Henrietta called in a panic and begged me to send her some money for an airplane ticket to get her out of Germany because 'they' were going to kill her."

"So, what did you do?" I asked.

She said, "I told her that she was acting crazy; that she lied to me during my entire life so why should I believe her now."

Karin sensed that my grandmother was simply a senile old woman who was now feeling guilty for what she had done to her. I told Karin about the phone call Tyler had just received. She said I shouldn't worry about it.

I told her how both times before that Henrietta asked, "Is this 864-2709?" And how we each answered "yes." And yet both times she said, "Sorry, wrong number," and immediately hung up.

I wanted Karin to understand that I felt that Henrietta's cryptic messages were informing me that she knew my number, but I needed to know hers - that my number was the "wrong" number but that if I knew the "right" number, I would find her and ultimately my mother.

My sense was that she might have had training as a secret agent. I became more concerned than ever that Henrietta could truly be in danger. But who would want to interrogate her or worse, hurt her, after all these years?

After some coaxing, Karin finally agreed to call her mother in Germany. I also contacted my friend Michael and asked him to call Henrietta as well. Both he and my mother tried calling Henrietta's home daily for two weeks straight. No one ever answered the phone.

About three weeks later, I received a call from Viola. She was at our mother's house. Karin was too upset to talk. Viola told me that our grandmother Henrietta was dead. Apparently, Karin's half-brother Hans had called to say that he had brought Henrietta to Turkey to live with him because she was senile and unable to care for herself. He told Karin that Henrietta had basically died of old age. He also said that he buried Henrietta's body in a grave he dug himself in the countryside outside Ankara, Turkey. He then boldly asked Karin to send a letter stating that she would not lay claim to Henrietta's estate. Karin asked for a copy of Henrietta's death certificate, but he said he didn't have one.

The whole thing upset my mother greatly; she didn't believe a word he was telling her and blamed herself for not reaching out to help her mother when she called. She asked Hans why he hadn't called earlier, but he had no response.

Several weeks later Karin called to tell me that Hans had called again. This time he asked that she help him pay for my grandmother's remaining bills, because all the money in her accounts was gone.

He had accused Karin of taking Henrietta's money while she was visiting in the United States. This confused Karin, because Henrietta didn't have any money or give any money to her.

Karin told me how Henrietta would just call from the airport in Atlanta without notice, asking for Karin to come pick her up. That seemed very odd as I wondered out loud if she had been somewhere else before that.

I reminded her that both of Henrietta's visits to the United States had taken place close to the same time as the mysterious phone calls I had received. This gave me reason to think that Henrietta's surprise visits to Karin could also be related to her spending patterns. I even brought up the idea that Henrietta had hired a private investigator to find me.

I asked Karin if Hans knew about me. She said, "No," and began crying on the phone. She said she was so sorry she hadn't believed Henrietta and how much she missed her. She also let me know that she had told Hans that she and Henrietta had begun to reconcile their differences and how much she needed to talk to her and how grateful she was that I was with her now.

I felt so bad for my mother.

I could hear the pain in her cries as she realized she would never hear her mother's voice again.

My head was spinning as I tried to make sense of this. Had my grandmother Henrietta knowingly put her life in danger by contacting me? Or could my life be in danger now for finding her?

I was wishing that Gertrude and John or my father Lonnie were here to shed some light on all of this. I knew one of them would know why Henrietta did what she did.

On December 3, 1994 I celebrated my first birthday with Karin in my life. Around 7 that evening, Karin called and wished me a happy birthday. Her voice sounded weak.

She said she had mailed me a birthday card but had forgotten to write in it. I hadn't received it and was feeling sad about all the birthdays we had missed together.

I offered to buy her a plane ticket to come visit me. She said, "No, I'm not feeling well and my stomach is bothering me, so I don't want to fly right now."

A few weeks later, my first Christmas card came with a note from my mother.

> *Laural,*
> *this is the first Christmas I have with you.*
> *December has always been the hardest time for me.*
> *I missed you so much.*
> *Every year was harder to be happy.*
> *But now I have you and know you*
> *and it makes my life complete.*
> *I wish to say so much but writing is hard for me.*
> *Have a very nice Christmas.*
> *I send you all my love.*
> *Mom.*

I held it close to my heart wishing I was with her right now so we could spend our first Christmas together. I made a promise with myself that I would go to Columbus and celebrate the holidays together with her next year.

Soon after New Year's Day, I had a dream that upset me. All day long it haunted me. I dreamt that Paul and I were on a black-and-white chessboard in a castle. There was a metal bed with a woman lying on it. Then she sat up and said my mom had called on the phone.

She said she couldn't understand the message, but it was something about my mom getting married to a man with a Middle Eastern sounding name.

Then I turned and saw Karin walking away from the castle over a mountain. She was wearing a cloak draped over her head, and I knew she was going to a Viking wedding. Everything in the dream was very dark and scary. When I woke up, I thought, "Viking wedding means Viking funeral." Why I do this I don't know, but I seem to use the word "wedding" when I am talking about a "funeral."

When I got home from work that day the answering machine was blinking. There was a message from Caroline asking me to call her. I called immediately.

In a shaking voice, Caroline explained that Mom was in the hospital with pancreatic cancer and that there was no cure - that our mother was going to die in a matter of weeks or possibly even days. I walked around the house in shock, before calling the airline to buy a one-way ticket to Atlanta.

How could I lose my mother whom I had just found? I had only seen her once, for two days total! I had only known of her for eight months; I should have known her for a lifetime! This wasn't fair. Karin was young, and we were both looking forward to many fun years together - sharing all the things a mother and daughter share. I was looking forward to her motherly advice and having her see her grandson, Tyler, grow up. I didn't sleep - I cried all night.

I arrived in Atlanta at 11:00 a.m. the next day.

My brother Lonnie was waiting for me at the gate. We hugged and he grabbed my hand to lead me through the airport. He then guided me to our mother's van, and we drove to Martin Army Hospital at Fort Benning.

I had forgotten what it felt like to be on a military base. The atmosphere was similar to that of my childhood, when we stayed for a short while at the Rhine Main Army/Air Base right before we came to the U.S.

Karin was on the eighth floor. I moved quickly through old, sterile corridors to the door of her small room. I walked in and there she was. Without thinking, I flew into her outstretched arms and sat on her bed. Her face was thin and pale, but she still had a beautiful smile. She hugged me with a twinkle in her eye. I pulled back and held her face in my hands, brushing the tears from her cheeks. She was even more beautiful than I remembered. Soon, I heard Viola and Caroline walk into the room. I got up and hugged both of them too. We were now all together again.

As the day went on, Karin's anxiety peaked. She was a serious chain-smoker and she needed a cigarette. The nurse on duty helped her up as we put her in a wheelchair, wrapping a blanket carefully around her. With an IV stand rolling behind her chair, we took her downstairs and outside for a cigarette. The air was warm for January – 60 degrees. It was the most peaceful moment of her day, and she was happy. Karin told us that she had accepted the fact that she was going to die, and that it was okay. Her life was now complete, we were all together and the secrets were released. It was time for her to be with her soulmate, Lonnie.

She told us she wanted to die at home, so we took her home the next day. Once in her own bed, our mother fell soundly asleep for the first time in days. She looked angelic lying in her black metal bed positioned at an angle facing the door. There was a small round marble table with an eccentric lamp of the Egyptian goddess Isis on it. Next to it was a black-and-white striped wing chair.

The other wall had a black dresser with an old television set and a black-and-white Victorian lamp with a young boy's face on the base. This lamp was always lit, as if the boy were her guardian angel. A bust of Apollo, the god of healing and prophecy, also stood watch in her room on top of her dresser. It all reminded me of the dream I had just a few days ago. I now understood that the dream had been an omen.

Later that evening she awoke and I was able to go into her room and talk with her alone. I brought her a first draft of this book. She was glad to see that I was moving forward. I assured her that I would tell our story with truth, integrity and love. She smiled and fell back to sleep.

The next morning, I woke up on the living room couch. It had rained earlier that morning, and the temperature had warmed to 75 degrees. It felt tropical outside. Karin woke up in a great mood, relaxed and content. I went into her bedroom and stayed with her. For the most part, I would just sit there quietly and hold her hand or get her something to drink. I brought her medicine and whatever she needed to be comfortable. I wanted to be with her as much as I possibly could. This was my only chance to absorb her presence into my soul.

That afternoon, Caroline and I went for a walk around the neighborhood. It was filled with upscale, historic homes built in the 1920s. The architecture had a romantic, southern style. Everywhere I looked was green and sensuous. Holly and English ivy crawled up trees and houses; the scent of honeysuckle filled the air.

Even the camellias were blooming!

It made me wonder what life would have been like growing up here. We came back to the house and sat on the porch while Karin was in her bedroom.

We greeted her friends and brought them into her room one at a time so they could talk with her. Karin wanted to introduce me to everyone.

She was so proud to tell them, "This is Laural, my daughter from Wisconsin." Many of her closest friends were gay men who absolutely adored her. They all left crying for they knew this was the last time they would see her alive.

I could feel their love and the impact she had on their lives. The reality of it all began sinking in.

I felt the need to get away and be by myself. I knew my mother was an avid gardener and that she had a little potting shed in the backyard. I thought this would be the perfect place to contemplate what was happening. Her wooden potting shed leaned against the garage like an old friend and was filled with clay pots, tools and watering cans. Karin's footsteps had worn the dirt floor into a surface that felt like hardened leather. I sat on the floor and gazed into her yard through screens that disappeared before my eyes.

A sweet, warm, gentle rain began to fall, softly waking up the garden around me. The air became intoxicating as my senses came alive. I felt the earth drinking in the moisture. I could see my mother's bedroom window above a row of white gardenia bushes. Her yard was magnificent, filled with green and white hostas, English ivy and an enchanting variety of perennials. Large drops of water hung onto everything in sight. The air was hot and humid as I took a few deep, delicious breaths and began to settle into the beauty of her garden.

I imagined myself living here, tending this garden with my mother. In that moment I felt my heart open and expand beyond my body as Karin's entire essence spontaneously entered my soul. Her life flashed in front of me and I instantly felt completely connected to her in spirit.

I began crying uncontrollably, harder and harder - simultaneously realizing that I was falling deeply in love with her and losing her at the same time. I ached to feel this sad yet sweet feeling for as long as I could. I was aware that this moment of rapture was fleeting, but it was so affirming to finally feel loved by her and to be able to truly love her back. I knew deep within me how I came to be in this world.

Karin was my mom and I was her daughter. She gave me life; together, she and my father had created me out of their profound love.

I had never felt that sense of connection before, so I stayed in that potting shed as long as I could trying to soak it all in. I didn't want to leave. I didn't want to stop crying, and I didn't want to stop feeling her presence inside of me. How unusual and profound it was to fill my heart with a lifetime of love in a few short minutes!

Next to me was a cement garden statue of a goose. I remember feeling that the goose had shared what I felt. I sat there next to that goose, looked at my mother's bedroom window and wondered how often she sat here talking to this exact goose. Mother Goose, I thought, how appropriate! All of this did seem a bit like a fairy tale.

From that moment on, I knew I could call Karin "Mom." It felt good inside to know she was my mom and that I loved her just as she loved me. I was excited to share this with her and feel the love we shared for each other. Eventually I composed myself and went back into the house to tell my mother about my experience in the potting shed. She smiled knowingly, looked at me with such immense clarity, and asked if I ever wondered how we could be so alike. She then asked me if I had ever felt a spirit with me.

"Yes, all the time," I said.

She went on, "Laural, you are so much like me because I raised you every day of your life. I would send my spirit out to you - my thoughts, my hopes, and my love - and you were able to receive them. Isn't that beautiful?"

She started talking to me about soul mates, explaining that Lonnie, my father, was her soul mate.

"Laural, I think Paul is also your soul mate." She went on to say how she believed that souls return to continue the work they left in their previous life.

She felt she was a very old soul and that this would be her last life on earth. She felt I was an old soul too, just like her, and that we had been together in many lifetimes before this one. My finding her brought closure to her soul in this lifetime. This was the first time I ever talked to anyone about reincarnation and previous lifetimes. It all made complete sense to me. I cried, realizing that my mother was validating a secret belief I had held deep within me. Everything she said confirmed what I felt within me and between us.

After that conversation with my mother, I called a florist in Wisconsin and ordered 13 red roses to be delivered to Paul at work. Today, January 30, 1995, was our 13th wedding anniversary, and it was the first time we had not been together to celebrate it. Plus, my mother had just reminded me of our connection as soul mates. I missed Paul and our son, Tyler; I wished they were here with me.

I went back into the room to be with Mom and continued our talk. She was rubbing her left shoulder as she told me that my father Lonnie was with her now. I asked her how she knew, "Your father always taps me on my left shoulder three times as a signal that he is with me." Mom whispered, "I'm ready to go. My dream has been fulfilled, for you have found me and you know your sisters and brother. Now your father is with me; my life is complete."

133

In that moment she began seizing, clutching her heart with her hands. I screamed for help. My brother Lonnie and Caroline's husband Brad rushed into the room. It was intense to see my brother scoop Mom into his arms as he carried her out to his car. They sped off to the hospital while the rest of us jumped in Caroline's van.

When we walked into the hospital's emergency door, an orderly came over to ask us what we needed. We told him our mother's name and that she had arrived just before us. The look on his face changed as he asked us to go into a nearby room. He told us that our mother was dead and there was nothing they could do.

She had signed a "do not resuscitate" order. We looked at each other in total disbelief. My body went numb as my heart ached to see her again. Everyone hugged the person they loved. I stood there silently holding the emptiness within me as tears poured out uncontrollably.

The orderly gently asked us if we wanted to see our mother. He warned us that she would look different to us and that her body was naked yet draped.

Without hesitation we said, "Yes."

He led us down a flight of stairs to a room. When he opened the door a cool rush of still air blew through my heart. My eyes instantly saw my mother's lifeless body lying on a stainless-steel table with only her face exposed.

I went over, kissed her forehead and prayed that her soul could hear me as I thanked her for loving me and waiting for me to find her. In the quiet recess of my heart, I knew that these few days we had shared were everything.

Later that evening, Viola wanted to talk to Lonnie, Caroline, and me alone. She told us that Mom had prepared a will the week before I came.

Viola explained that Mom had willed me one of her most precious possessions – her anniversary ring from our father.

Viola said, "Mom wanted you to have this ring as a constant reminder that you were loved by both a mother and a father." Time stood still as Viola handed me my mother's precious gift. As I held it for the first time, I saw that it was made of soft rose-colored gold that seemed to be birthing a platinum orb.

Seven small diamonds were embedded into the orb like stars forming an infinity symbol. It was very mystical and reminded me of the eye of the Universe.

Then the awareness of receiving my mother's anniversary ring on my 13th wedding anniversary rushed through me. This day would now and forever be changed. It now marked the anniversary of my mother's death and the beginning of my life with Paul.

I later learned that it was also the day Hitler took power in 1933, the year Karin was born, in Germany.

As I slid her ring on the finger of my right hand, I felt this sacred connection to her that seemed to go beyond this lifetime. I glanced at my wedding ring on my left hand and how this diamond was the one my father John had given my mother Gertrude. It was so beautiful to know they were all with me in spirit, right within my reach.

I was also given the cement goose from the potting shed, the guardian angel lamp next to her bed, a bronze statue holding a bird, along with the bust of Apollo, a tapestry rug and my mother's menorah. These gifts provided a physical connection to the mysterious woman who gave me life.

I could feel through them her connection to the world of esoteric knowledge. I saw her not only as my mother but also as my teacher.

It was a simple ceremony. Viola, Caroline and Lonnie asked me to write Mom's eulogy. They felt I understood her soul. Her unlit menorah stood silently next to the urn that held her ashes. We handed out red AIDS ribbons to everyone who attended in support of the gay community she loved so dearly. She had been an activist who stood with them in marches and nursed those who died from AIDS. She knew firsthand, based on her life in Nazi Germany, that she needed to act. I felt proud to be her daughter.

I reflected on how differently my mother Gertrude felt toward gay people. I flashed back to the summer of 1975, a few weeks after Gertrude had thrown my adoption papers at me saying she wished she had never adopted me because I was a "bad seed" who turned out just like my mother. Now she was calling to tell me that she was coming to see me and would be at my place in Eau Claire by 1:00 that day! I nervously waited for her arrival, and wondering if she was going to apologize for what she said to me. She was usually very punctual, so when the time was 2:00 I began to worry. Eventually I went downstairs from my apartment and found her sitting in her car with the windows rolled up!

I asked, "What are you doing out here?"

She said, "I'm not getting out of my car with that 'thing' sitting there."

I glanced over and realized she was referring to my friend, a gay man with long blonde hair and purple nail polish. He was sitting on a bench near the front door. I told her his name and that he is my friend and that she should come in so we can talk. She refused to get out and drove away. I immediately turned around and apologized to my friend who overheard the entire conversation. I was upset, embarrassed that Gertrude could be so cruel. And now here I am at Karin's funeral surrounded by gay men.

After Karin's service, Viola, Caroline, Lonnie and myself walked silently carrying her ashes through the winding paths of this tree-lined cemetery in Georgia. We set Mom's urn into the ground next to our father.

They were finally together again.

A headstone etched with their names marked their final resting place. It was serene as an American flag stood at attention under the shade of an old oak tree.

My mind flashed to the horse pasture where we had scattered John and Gertrude's ashes. Neither had a headstone with their names etched in it or an American flag to mark their final resting place. I felt sad for them and wondered how different this could have been had they told me the truth before they died.

What I did know was that all four of my parents were etched in my heart and that I was determined to better understand what had happened to each of them and to me.

*"I surrendered my beliefs
and found myself at the tree of life
injecting my story into the veins of leaves
only to find that stories like forests
are subject to seasons"*
- Saul Williams -

CHAPTER 10: THE TREE OF LIFE

It was now 1997, and two years had passed since Karin's death. I was trying to write this story to honor the promise I made to her, but I only had a hundred handwritten pages so far. Bill, a copywriter and friend, offered to input what I had into a computer file. He encouraged me to keep writing because it was an important story.

My life was busy; we were maintaining 40 acres of land in the country and remodeling our home. Paul commuted to Algoma every day for his job at Jag Outdoor, while I drove to Goltz and Associates in Green Bay. Tyler was an active 13-year-old. We were also coaching his Pony League baseball team and converting 25 acres of corn field into prairie and woodland through the CRP (Conservation Reserve Program) by hand planting 300 oak and pine trees.

I had taken a few days off from work to renovate our home when the phone rang. It was Kris, our CFO, letting me know that I had been awarded the Silver Medal Award from the National Advertising Federation, which is quite an honor. This award is based on outstanding contributions in the field of advertising as well as a person's commitment to their community. I could hear the staff clapping in the background. I wished I were there to share in this moment. I went to the office the next day. Bob Goltz was sitting behind his desk, but I was running late for an appointment with the local extension office to file our CRP crop report.

I casually yelled, "Hi Bob, see you later!"

The following morning the phone rang and this time it was Ellen, our vice president.

She told me that Bob was missing and presumed dead. Apparently, he left the office shortly after I saw him. He went home and took a handgun from his dresser drawer and walked away. No one had seen him since.

I dropped everything to run to the agency. By the time I arrived I saw staff members crying, my heart sank. It was confirmed that he died by suicide. In a state of shock, we gathered the staff together and shared what we knew. We went into crisis mode for several days as we informed our clients, vendors and the press of what had happened and what the funeral arrangements were. It was both a tragedy and an honor to apply all of our resources and skills to help Bob's family during this incredibly difficult time.

There were hundreds of people at his funeral; he was greatly admired as a leader in our community. His death was a shock to everyone and we found ourselves trying to explain what had happened to those who asked. Bob had been silently suffering from depression and very few people knew it. He was good at hiding it, like so many others.

Later, at his graveside service, we were standing under a blossoming cherry tree on a beautiful spring day. As Bob's casket was lowered into the ground, a gentle gust of wind released thousands of soft pink petals that rained upon us. This fleeting moment of beauty felt like a blessing from Bob as we said our last goodbyes.

Our agency began creating ways to educate the public on the links between depression and suicide. We researched organizations to partner with and discovered a national organization called SAVE (Suicide Awareness Voices of Education). We launched a multi-pronged suicide awareness campaign and partnered with local organizations.

A few weeks after his death I found myself standing in front of a crowded room of advertising professionals to accept the Silver Medal Award. I was terrified but focused.

Bob had been the first to receive this award in our community, which made it even more intense. He was my boss, my mentor and my friend. This was supposed to be a shared celebration, but instead it felt like a eulogy. I reflected on the loss I was feeling and the lessons I had received, not only from Bob but also from my parents.

With Bob's sudden death our agency was now at risk. We had been progressively growing since I arrived in 1992 and this had been our best year in both morale and revenue. I, along with two others, submitted an offer to purchase the agency from Bob's estate, based on the valuation from our accounting firm, but it was rejected. Instead, they froze our spending and put the agency up for sale. After six months of being held hostage, we purchased the agency by merging with Seering & Company and renamed ourselves Goltz-Seering. In January of 1998 I was asked to be the president/creative director. This was the same title Bob Goltz had held. It was an honor and a huge responsibility. My life went into overdrive as the agency continued to grow. My dream of writing this book and fulfilling my life's purpose now seemed frivolous and self-indulgent.

On the morning of September 11, 2001, I was listening to the news on NPR as I drove into work. When I heard about the first plane hitting the Twin Towers I was alarmed. By the time I walked into my office and turned on the TV, the second plane had hit and I was scared. I called the staff together as we witnessed the unbelievable events that were unfolding in real time. We were all in shock.

The next morning, I stood in the shower pleading with the Universe for guidance on what to do. I felt this was a wake-up call for our world and for me personally. I was praying for my Tree Spirit to appear to me, because I felt people really needed to understand each other better.

Tears were washing over me when I felt a sensation softly float down my spine. I turned around and saw her in front of me. She filled the space with her translucent nature. Her gaze was sweet and familiar. It had been exactly forty years since I last saw her as a child in Germany. I instantly felt that she was revealing herself to me as the Tree of Life. My body became electric as I welcomed her into my soul like a long-lost friend. I knew she had returned to help me heal my broken heart as well as the world around me.

I sensed it was time for me to fulfill my purpose. It was as if everything that had happened in my life had prepared me for this moment. I entered a new stage of understanding that inspired me to search deeper into the roots of world belief. My mind flashed on the events that were unfolding. The entire world was now aware that Islamic fundamentalists had taken responsibility for the attacks. I sensed the fear and confusion regarding the lack of understanding between Christians, Jews and Muslims. The anger and blame simmering in this collective melting pot was getting ready to explode and I wanted to help.

I recalled the story of Adam and Eve being cast out of the Garden of Eden and forbidden to eat from the Tree of Life because they ate from the Tree of Knowledge of Good and Evil. I thought, how odd that knowledge was wrong and that we were punished for wanting to know more. I knew in that moment that I needed to become as knowledgeable as I could. There was a voice deep within me that kept saying, "It's time for you to learn and begin to teach. This is how you will help people understand each other better."

From that point on, I began researching the origins of world belief from 40,000 BCE to present day. My passion soon became an obsession as I tried to unravel the stories that tore us apart in hopes of bringing us together again.

142

I quickly learned that it wasn't easy to find unbiased information on various religions. They were riddled with dogma, personal agendas and eons of patriarchal power.

I created a simple timeline to help me keep it all in sequential order by drawing a tree that branched out into different belief systems. I saw the tree with seven roots representing each of the seven major continents. The base of the trunk represented all of the indigenous belief systems that existed throughout the world before religions were formed. It was from this unified trunk that the major branches began to emerge, as each culture created its own unique and sometimes polarizing creation stories. It soon became clear that we were all interrelated for we share the same roots. As we moved into different lands, our ancestors told stories of how they came to be. These stories laid the foundations that formed each of the world's major religions.

The Tree of Life is a metaphor for our ancestral family tree. Over time we lost the original stories of our ancestors and became disconnected from our nature-based roots. It was confirming to learn how most belief systems involved a tree in their creation story. My purpose now was to untangle the roots so I could see the bigger picture. It was an exciting time as I learned that anthropologists were mapping the human genome and how all humans are believed to have originated in Africa over 200,000 years ago.

I found myself drawn to the mystery teachings of the Kabbalah, also known as the Tree of Life in Jewish mysticism. It represents a path for healing the wound of separation between humans knowing themselves and their eternal soul. I researched indigenous cultures that saw trees as connectors to the past, present, and future where ancestral spirits provided guidance for their tribe: for example, the story of Buddha achieving enlightenment by sitting under a Bodhi tree and realizing that suffering was a choice.

These stories resonated deep within me as I reflected on the Tree Spirit in Germany. I searched for information on trees and the spiritual practices of ancient European people.

I discovered that many Europen cultures worshipped trees as benevolent beings. The Proto-Indo-European (PIE) words *daru* (tree, integrity/truth) and *vid* (wisdom) inspired the word Druid. In turn the oak family of trees, which included beech and chestnut, were named *duir,* which also meant *door*. Druids were known as the wisdom keepers and teachers who knew how to access with wisdom of trees. The Anglo-Saxon word *treo,* (tree/truth) evolved into *tree*.

In Greek mythology the oak tree was named *drys*. The spirit or nymph of an oak tree was known as a *dryad*. This fascinated me because *dryads* were female guardians of the trees they inhabited, and when the tree died the *dryad* died along with it. I wondered if the Tree Spirit was a *dryad*.

I tried to remember the type of tree that the Tree Spirit showed herself in; maybe it was an oak. I began searching through photos of trees, to jog my memory.

In modern classification, oak, beech and chestnut all belong to the *Fagaceae* (beech) family.

I felt my heart longing to reconnect to Holzhausen Park and to the tree that captured my imagination so long ago. I had been wanting to go back to Germany ever since we left, but my mother Gertrude never wanted to discuss it. Now I was a busy mom, wife and business owner. I also didn't know how to speak German or had anyone in Germany to visit.

This dream pulled at my heart and never let go. I patiently waited for a sign to make this dream come true.

CHAPTER 11: THE SHIFT

I was enjoying the sounds of ice and snow trickling off our roof, when suddenly the phone rang. It was Henry, my adoptive brother, calling about an unexpected letter he had just received and he didn't know what to do with it.

"The mailman just put a letter in my mailbox addressed to Gertrude Virtues, Algoma, WI," he said.

"Who is it from?" I asked, intrigued.

"It looks like Luci and Heinz," Henry responded.

My heart leapt with pure joy, as I yelled, "That's Sisi. She and Heinz have finally found us!"

I immediately drove to Henry's house to pick up the letter. Once I arrived, I clutched the letter to my heart and thanked the Universe for this gift. I opened it but I couldn't read it. It was written entirely in German.

Fortunately, I had met Sabine, a foreign exchange student from Germany, who shadowed me at work a few months before. We had become friends and she was more than willing to help me with my translation needs. I typed each letter in the note and sent it to her via e-mail. That day in March 2004 she responded with the translation:

Dear Family Virtues, how are you? I have written to you so many times and never heard anything. Please let me hear something from you. Please send me your telephone number and we will call you. Dear Mrs. Virtues! All the best for your birthday, a lot of luck and health. That's what our wishes are for you.

Loving greetings, Sisi and Heinz

Wow, I thought. Gertrude died 15 years ago and Sisi didn't know that? Had my mother secretly been writing to Sisi before she died? Had she lied to me about this too?

I was confused yet so excited to finally be in touch with them. My heart swelled with anticipation.

I immediately wrote a letter for Sabine to translate.

It was so bizarre to think I was receiving hand-written letters written in German and rewriting them letter by letter via e-mail to Sabine in Germany only to have her rewrite it in English. I could then read it and respond so she could write my response in German. From there I could print it and mail it back to Germany. I was so grateful for all of it. In my first letter to Sisi and Heinz I told them of all that had happened, and when both of our parents had passed.

Sisi replied:

Dear Laural! Finally, we hear from you, thank you. It was my biggest wish to know what has become of you and how you are. The first night after we received your letter we could not sleep because of both happiness and sadness. When you went to America in 1961 we were still in Frankfurt until 1988. Yes, dear Laural, we are now 75 years old and we are still healthy. We never had children though. Dear Laural, unfortunately I do not speak any English, which is really a pity otherwise we could talk on the phone. Do you and Henry have memories of us at all?? Now my beloved Laural, the best regards for today.

Yours, Sisi and Heinz

I was stunned and thrilled. I knew that their letter was an invitation for me to reconnect with my past to help me move forward. It had been 45 years since I left Germany as a child, but my memories of Sisi were vivid and real.

I thought of all the times I ached for her and yet she questioned if I remembered her. I didn't understand how this could be.

I also wondered why they didn't have children. I felt in my heart that we were loved as if we were their own children and how healing this was for them, as it was for me. I called my brother Henry, and told him about the letter. I asked him if he remembered Sisi and Heinz, but he said no.

I was sad for him that he had no memory of Germany and our childhood there. I didn't let this dampen my enthusiasm as I began to create a plan that would allow me to visit Sisi and Heinz and retrace my steps back to the Tree Spirit in Holzhausen Park.

I felt that by doing this I could get answers to some of the questions I had been searching for.

With the help of Sabine, we continued to write back and forth; learning and sharing what was happening in our lives. Sisi was hesitant to answer any of my questions about my birth parents or my adoption.

I could sense she was protecting my parents John and Gertrude. She would always remind me of how amazing they both were, how smart and good they were to her and Heinz. She was very loyal to them. I knew I would need to meet with her in person to ask the tough questions.

From that moment I began planning a way to finally go back to my childhood home, to see Sisi and Heinz and to retrace the steps that had brought me here.

*"Except during the nine months
before he draws his first breath
no man manages his affairs
as well as a tree does."*
- George Bernard Shaw -

CHAPTER 12 – THE PREPARATION

It was 2005, I had just turned 50 and was struggling trying to lead the double life that was tearing me apart. It had been ten years since my mother Karin had passed away, and seven since Bob Goltz had died. To most of my co-workers, family and friends, I was a successful businesswoman, wife, mother, and community activist.

But deep inside I was also a little girl from Frankfurt, Germany who was desperately trying to heal the heart break and confusion that haunted me.

I was experiencing intense panic attacks, insomnia, migraine headaches, asthma and IBS. My doctor diagnosed me with PTSD and was concerned about the stress I was placing on myself and what it was doing to my health.

His recommendation was counseling.

I began seeing a therapist on a weekly basis. After sharing my entire life story with her, she suggested that I was a second-generation survivor of WWII.

The more we talked, the more I felt myself plummeting into a very dark place. I knew that I wouldn't be able to help others until I healed the story that was holding me. She believed that I needed to cut back at work. I agreed, but I didn't know how I could do that.

During one of my sessions, I told my therapist that I would have to wait two more years before leaving my job. I'll never forget that moment when she placed her hand firmly on my knee and looked me straight in the eyes.

"Laural, you don't have two more years," she said.

My heart sank as the intensity in her eyes made me fear that I could die if I didn't do something now, and that something was to leave my career and face my life.

This felt similar to what the heart specialist told me when I was a VISTA volunteer. I knew she was right, but releasing my ownership and leaving the agency was much more complicated than she knew. But having Sisi and Heinz back in my life gave me the courage to move forward.

Unfortunately, life didn't go exactly as I had hoped. The economy was beginning to falter and several of our largest clients had merged or been restructured. In each case they moved their corporate headquarters out of state. Within a matter of months, we lost 50% of our revenue, which caused us to drastically downsize the agency. I offered to step down but my offer was denied. Instead, the principal partner we had merged with decided to resign, we renamed our agency - Infusion Inc.

At a time when I was hoping to reduce my stress, I found myself under increasing pressure to secure new accounts along with retaining and managing the accounts we had. To complicate things our banking partner demanded a "freeze" on our personal assets, or they would "call" our loan. This meant I could lose my initial investment as well as all the money I had reinvested into the agency. Undeterred, I continued to move forward, even though my financial situation was tenuous at best.

Paul and I decided to downsize. In May 2006, we sold our 40-acre Garden of Eden and moved into Green Bay. Fortunately, we had set enough money aside for Paul, Tyler and me to travel to Europe and visit with Sisi and Heinz. Tyler had been living in San Diego with his band Sweet Genius and was now moving to Asheville, NC, to study herbalism. He had timed his trip so he could help us move.

On June 6, 2006 I told my two partners that my last day at the agency would be July 7, 2007.

In December 2006 I celebrated my 52nd birthday. Paul surprised me with a trip to New York City, the exact city that marked my official entrance into the United States.

New York City was all dressed up for the holidays. The sights and sounds of Christmas and Rockefeller Center filled the air as snowflakes gently fell from the sky. I was thrilled to discover a *Christkindlmarkt*, a German outdoor market, at the entrance to Central Park. We strolled through open-air shops filled with German ornaments, candies and cookies. I felt magically transported back to Frankfurt as a child. We boarded a horse drawn carriage to tour the park. The sound of horse's hooves clopping on the ground created a soothing ride. They became silent at the edge of Strawberry Field. We left the comfort of the carriage and walked inside the Imagine Memorial to honor John Lennon. Tears rolled from my eyes as I silently thanked him for inspiring my soul and his gifts to the world. Flowers were strewn everywhere as people were preparing for the anniversary of his death on December 8th. We decided to take a taxi to the harbor where the SS United States had docked 45 years earlier. As we drove through the streets of lower Manhattan, I could feel the open wound of 9/11. We drove by the site where the Twin Towers once stood. Excavators and cranes now stood in its footprint. I sensed the sadness and the desire to heal. The Statue of Liberty stood strong gazing with quiet resolve.

After our whirlwind weekend we flew to Asheville, North Carolina to pick up Tyler and his stuff. We stayed at the Biltmore hotel, which was magnificent. We rented a U-Haul truck and drove to Green Bay. Tyler was moving in with us before going to New Zealand for a 3-month herbal apprenticeship with Isla Burgess. In April we would travel as a family to Europe for three weeks. Afterward he would be going to the Northeast School of Botanical Medicine.

It was great to have Tyler home again, at least for a while. We talked about our future as well as our hopes and dreams. We found ourselves both at a crossroads.

I was reading *Soul Retrieval* by Sandra Ingerman.

"Are you interested in shamanism?" Tyler asked.

"I don't know" I replied, "But I'm fascinated by the concept of soul retrieval and how a person's soul can detach during times of trauma. When they lose a part of their soul, they call it soul loss. Repeated soul loss can cause people to become anxious or depressed, which can manifest into emotional and physical ailments. This might explain why I have panic attacks and anxiety. I think I want to learn how to do this and retrieve my lost soul parts."

"Mom, I think this is your 'calling'," Tyler stated.

His words resonated within me, so I began researching how people knew if they have been "called" and what that really meant. I soon discovered that trees are one of the oldest ways of being called in shamanic tradition. The Universe couldn't have been clearer as the Tree Spirit etched itself deeper into my psyche. Tyler encouraged me to explore the Four Winds Society created by Dr. Alberto Villoldo, a psychologist who studied PTSD and how it effects our mind, body and soul. I read his biography, and was fascinated to see that he had studied with indigenous Andean healers in Peru. Even though his work focused on the Andean cosmology, he incorporated other healing modalities and world beliefs along with Jungian psychology into his curriculum.

A few days later, during the dark morning hours of February, I had a very vivid and lucid dream of a large crow sitting on my right arm cawing directly into my ear: "Laural! Laural! Laural!" I felt the weight of it on my arm, and it was beginning to hurt.

I tried to wake myself so I could shoo the crow away. By the time I awoke I realized it was just a dream, but I could still feel its presence on my arm. It seemed like an omen of some sort. I wanted to understand why the crow came to me in my dream. I searched the internet for information and discovered that crows remind us to listen and be authentic with ourselves as we move forward.

So, there it was - a very real reminder that this was exactly what I was supposed to do. From that day on, crow became a faithful reminder for me to be honest with myself as I began to walk this new path. Many days, at just the right moment, a crow would find me and begin cawing at me until I acknowledged it. There were three crows that took up residence in our yard. A few days after this "calling," my mind wrestled with how to bring my research on world religions together. I realized that my original idea of a simple graphic was becoming very complicated. It was then that I had a vision of the Tree of Life within a circle.

The word "mandala" echoed in my heart. I immediately searched the internet for information on mandalas and discovered Dr. Judith Cornell, author of *Mandala: Luminous Symbols for Healing, Drawing the Light from Within: Keys to Awaken your Creative Power* and *Amma: Healing the Heart of the World.*

I sent an email and she responded immediately! I shared my desire to understand the roots of world belief and the revelation given to me by a Tree Spirit. She told me about a silent five-day mandala retreat based on each of the world's major religions, that she was facilitating that August.

She was also beginning to offer a two-year mandala facilitator training program, which required attending two week-long intensives and completing 108-hours of actual facilitation.

The following day I received an e-mail from a friend who attended the local Unitarian Universalist Church in Manitowoc, Wisconsin. She told me that a graduate of the Four Winds was going to be the guest speaker on Sunday and she wanted to know if I would like to come. Tyler and I both wanted to meet him. As it turned out he wasn't there to talk about his studies, but to read his poetry. Michael's spirit was gentle and humble. After the service was over, we stayed to talk with him. I learned that he had just finished the Medicine Wheel portion of The Four Winds training and he was eager to share his thoughts. When I looked at The Four Winds website, I discovered that a two-year Medicine Wheel program along with the Healing the Light Body practitioner training was being held in Madison, Wisconsin that spring of 2007! The Medicine Wheel portion was made up of four, 3.5-day sessions based on the four directions (south, west, north, east). The Healing the Light Body practitioner training involved four, 3.5-day classes that followed the Medicine Wheel. All eight of those programs would be in Wisconsin. To be certified as an energy medicine practitioner, I would also need to attend three week-long master classes in Park City, Utah, and facilitate twelve private sessions.

I felt that my direction had found me, and I was ready to act on it. I signed up for both programs without hesitation.

I sensed that shamanic healing would help heal on a personal level and the mandala would open me to collective understanding. I also saw myself combining mandalas with shamanic-based wisdom to create a healing path for others!

I had no idea what to expect regarding shamanic healing so I scheduled a session with Michael, which he offered to do for free the very next day.

I went to his home where he had his healing practice. He asked me to identify my intention for the session.

"I want to release the fear that is holding me," I said.

He had me lie down fully clothed on a massage table. I noticed that the room was filled with stones, crystals, feathers, rattles and other sacred objects. Michael smudged the room with sage and lit a candle. He then had me choose a stone from his *mesa* (medicine bundle) and asked me to blow my intention into the stone to set my intention.

He placed the stone onto my heart and encouraged me to breathe and allow myself to see and feel the fear that was holding me. As I started breathing I suddenly sensed a sharp pain in my sternum. I told him about the pain and he asked me to try to identify it. I tried to imagine what it was.

"It feels like a big metal whaling hook," I said.

"Whom does this hook belong to?" he inquired.

I continued breathing, trying to understand why this big hook was stuck in my chest and whom it was from. I began sensing that it belonged to my father Lonnie, which I thought was crazy since I wasn't thinking of him at all.

"I feel like this hook belongs to my father Lonnie whom I have never met," I said in a sense of disbelief.

"Do you want to remove the hook?" he asked.

"Yes," I replied.

Even though it wasn't an actual physical hook, it felt very real and the pain was becoming more intense.

He asked me if I wanted pull it out myself since it was related to my father. As I tugged on it, I could feel that it was also stuck in my heart. The more I envisioned the shape of the hook and where it was, the easier it was to begin pulling it out. As the hook began to release from my chest, I felt the sensation of bleeding profusely. I lifted my head to look at my chest and saw nothing.

When I relaxed and set my head back down on the table, I immediately felt a large energetic sea turtle floating above me. Eventually the turtle lay directly over my heart, which stopped the feeling that I was bleeding.

"Do you need anything?" Michael asked quizzically.

"No, I got the hook out and now a turtle is helping me so I just want to lie here and connect with her," I said.

Within a few minutes I sensed her dropping a single luminous egg into my heart before she gently disappeared.

"I think I'm all done now," I stated, "I was just gifted an egg to help me heal the hole in my heart."

I asked him if this was what sessions were like, because that was really weird!

He said it wasn't "normal" but that each one was different. He also explained that I had basically facilitated my own healing, which showed him that I was more than ready for the Four Winds practitioner training.

Even though this was all very new and interestingly strange, I felt that I had been given an actual gift by the turtle, but what it was, I wasn't quite sure. This session seemed to access an entirely different realm of reality that was amazing. I was skeptical yet intrigued, because it all felt very, very real, but was it real or was it just my imagination?

CHAPTER 13 – THE REUNION

I had been making plans for our family trip to Europe for over a year. We had decided to spend one week in Frankfurt, one week in Paris, and one week in Amsterdam.

My priorities were to see Sisi and Heinz, to go to Holzhausen Park and find my tree, plus visit my childhood home. I had no idea who lived in the house now, but I was able to get a telephone number using an online directory.

I called, Dr. Hazel Stroth answered, and I soon learned that she was originally from South Dakota. Hazel told me how she and her husband, Dr. Rolph Stroth, had bought the house from the U.S. government in 1962 – soon after we moved out. They had been living there ever since. Hazel had many questions for me, since she had always sensed it was a "spook" house, meaning a U.S. spy house. She asked why the windows were all blacked out in the attic and why there were heavy-duty electrical hookups. I told her that my father had been a CIA agent and that his unit was headquartered there. I also let her know that my mother developed and edited film in the attic. Over the next few months, we wrote back and forth. I discovered that she was a journalist for the *Stars and Stripes*. I also learned that they had lost their only two daughters in an accident. I wondered how it felt for her to hear my voice?

When I asked her about Holzhausen Park, her response surprised me. "Oh yes," she said. "That park has many spirits in it. The trees are full of them." She went on to say that recently, several really large, old trees had been cut down after being hit by lightning or dying of old age.

Some of those trees were thought to have been nearly 600 years old. I hoped and prayed that my tree wasn't one of them. Hazel was a kindred spirit, full of curiosity. I felt that destiny had brought us together and they had been holding and protecting this house for me to come back to, so I could visit it again.

We boarded the plane to Frankfurt on April 2nd, 2007, the 18th anniversary of Gertrude's death. I was finally going home to Germany, something my heart had been yearning to do for 45 years. So many emotions and thoughts were flooding through me as I began to reflect on my mothers and fathers and how often they had made this same trip. I thought ahead to Sisi and Heinz, wondering what I might learn and seeing their faces in person.

When we arrived in Frankfurt, a taxi was waiting to take us to our hotel. After we checked in, I called another cab to take us to Holzhausen Park. The taxi driver drove down Oder Weg and turned onto Fürstenburger Str.

When I saw the street sign, I got all excited and said, "This is the street I grew up on."

"Where?" asked the driver, sounding surprised.

"2 Fürstenburger Strasse." I said.

"It's right here," he said.

I looked out the window and there was the house, just as grand as I remembered. Since it was right on the corner, I asked him to let us out. I couldn't believe it. I was finally standing in front of my childhood home. Tyler and Paul seemed awestruck with how beautiful and large it was. I looked to my left, and there was Holzhausen Park only a few steps away. As we walked to the park, tears welled up in my eyes. My heart began to swell in gratitude for this moment. Everything was familiar and soothing and beautiful.

It was a perfect spring day in April with the sun shining through the trees, buds were just beginning to form. The grass was green and the air was fresh. Tulips and daffodils were pushing their way through the ground. The birds were singing, all of my senses came alive. I loved this park so dearly. The feel of the park took me instantly back in time. I also noticed that many of the trees I remembered as a child were gone. As I looked at the castle standing in the middle of the moat, I realized that the beautiful white trumpeter swans were gone as well. We walked on the cobblestone walkway that led to dirt paths into the trees. I searched and searched for my tree, retracing my steps and trying to remember exactly where I was when I first met the Tree Spirit forty-five years ago.

But I couldn't seem to find the tree.

When I sensed I found the spot, I realized that the tree was no longer there. What I did see was bare ground and lots of large tree trunks, almost four feet wide, lying on their sides marking the edges of the paths. I walked along and touched each one of them, hoping to feel a connection, but there was none. It seemed as if their life force was sleeping and I was having a hard time connecting to it. At first, I was devastated, but I didn't cry. I had been dreaming of this day forever. I had imagined caressing the bark of the tree with my hands and feeling its spirit again within my heart.

As I stood there breathing in the spring air, I began to understand that the spirit of the tree was within me even though the actual tree was gone. I felt that she was like my power animal, similar to how I felt about bears and crows. In essence, I came to realize that my constitutional make-up was similar to a tree. As I bowed my head to honor the ground where the tree once stood, I noticed a sweet little golden stone shaped like a triangle at my feet. I picked it up and thanked the tree and the park for this special gift.

I decided to keep the stone as a way to honor the journey that brought me here. We left the park and walked past my house once again, then down Oeder Weg to our hotel. We passed the bakery I loved as a child, and I couldn't resist; I went inside, and there were the almond cookies I adored. I bought some for all of us. They were absolutely delicious. As we continued walking, I felt so at home and totally alive. I had never felt this way about anyplace else in the world. This place was perfect for me. Trees, parks, cobblestone streets, history, comfort, walking distance to shops and markets, fresh cheese, sausage, fruits, vegetables...what more could a person want? Before long we were downtown and back at our hotel. I began to feel as if I had never left. To be able to come back and see this all again was like a miracle. The childhood I dreamed of and left behind had been waiting for me to come home.

Sisi and Heinz showed up at our hotel early the next morning. They did not speak English, but their eyes spoke volumes. As soon as I saw Sisi's face, I felt her love. Heinz looked a little tired, but he was clearly happy to finally be together again. I had arranged for Sabine to join us and help translate; when she arrived, we all sat together in the tiny lobby of the hotel and talked. Sisi had so much she wanted to tell me, and so many questions she wanted to ask.

"I lived with Mr. and Mrs. Virtues as a housemaid before you were born. Mr. Virtues was a very important person in Frankfurt, over one hundred agents worked for him. Everyone looked up to him and saw what a sweet, good man he was. Mrs. Virtues was a tough person but I respected her intelligence, determination and creative talents. Mr. and Mrs. Virtues told people that they wanted to adopt a baby girl and when they heard about you, Mrs. Virtues was so excited. You were given to them right after you were born. You were so small and Mrs. Virtues was very happy."

"But then she learned that your mother was in jail, and she told me that she did not want to adopt you anymore because you were a bad seed," Sisi continued.

I thought back to that day when Gertrude called me a bad seed and threw my adoption papers at me. Now I understood its true origins.

"Someone came and talked to Mrs. Virtues and tried to calm her down by telling her that your mother was not in jail for being a criminal. Instead your mother was arrested for being a vagrant. When Mrs. Virtues learned that, she was more comfortable and decided to adopt you. She finally allowed herself to believe that you were the daughter she had always dreamed of, but then she learned that your mother did not want to give you up for adoption. Your birth mother wanted Mr. and Mrs. Virtues to only be your foster parents until she got out of jail," Sisi said.

My mind began piecing the puzzle together as this was consistent with what Karin had told me.

"Mrs. Virtues cried every day for months, because she was afraid that you would be taken away from her. After many months, Mrs. Virtues hired a lawyer to talk to your mother in jail and convince her to sign the adoption papers," Sisi said.

I reflected on how my mother, Karin, had told me about a lawyer who came into her jail cell and threatened her. She felt so helpless when he said that she would not get out of jail until she signed the release papers.

My heart dropped as I realized that it was actually my mother Gertrude who had forced Karin to give me up against her will. How could she have done this to Karin and to me? Sisi could see the expression on my face change to disbelief as she placed her hand on my knee to comfort me.

"Tell me Laural, when did you learn about your adoption?" Sisi asked.

161

I fought back the tears and emotions within me as I tried to answer her questions without sounding angry.

"I accidently discovered that I was adopted when I found a postcard at my grandmother's house the day before I started third grade. I asked my mother Gertrude what it meant, but she refused to talk to me about it. Every time I brought it up, she would get very mad and upset with me. I didn't learn anything until I was 20 years old," I said.

"What happened when you were 20?" Sisi asked.

"I was in college and Gertrude found my birth control pills. She started yelling at me that she never should have adopted me because I was a bad seed. She threw my adoption papers at me so I could learn for myself that my mother was a drunken prostitute," I said.

Sisi became visibly upset, shaking her head.

"Didn't Mrs. Virtues understand that all girls take birth control pills?" I shook my head no as I felt Sisi's love.

"I don't understand," said Sisi. "Mrs. Virtues promised me that she would tell you about your mother as soon as you were old enough to ask. I can't believe she didn't tell you. Why didn't she tell you? Why did she do this to you?"

Now Sisi seemed angry and confused by this and conveyed in German what she had just heard to Heinz. I could see in their faces how upset they both were to hear how things had turned out.

"Why do you think Mrs. Virtues acted this way?"

"I think everything changed when my biological father Lonnie claimed me and my older sister Viola as his daughters. He was asked to come to the Provost Marshall's office to discuss the situation because my mother Karin had signed unconditional release papers."

"When this happened, it set off a chain reaction that may have blown my father John's cover," I said.

Sisi was shocked, as she was not aware of this at all, which really surprised me. She seemed to know nothing of my birth father Lonnie. I asked her if she knew anything regarding why we left Germany in the first place.

"Everything happened really fast because Mr. Virtues' unit was suddenly shut down and you left. Both Mr. and Mrs. Virtues asked Heinz and me to move with them to the United States. I wanted to go with you so I could be with you and Henry, but Heinz didn't want to leave Germany," Sisi said as she glanced at Heinz.

I saw the sadness in Heinz's face. He looked like he was going to start crying.

Sisi continued at a rapid pace as Sabine translated.

"I wrote many letters to Mrs. Virtues after you left, and in the beginning she wrote back. But after you moved to Algoma, Mrs. Virtues stopped writing to me. I didn't understand why, so I kept writing several times a year, every year. I never gave up hope. Then you, my dear Laural, finally wrote back to me. I was so afraid I had lost you and that I was never going to see you or know what happened to you," Sisi said.

Sisi began crying as Heinz put his arm around her and tried to console her. It was heartbreaking to see how devastated Sisi felt losing Henry and me so quickly and then never having children of her own.

It was now very clear to me how much we actually meant to her. Feelings of anger and confusion began growing in my heart as I realized that my mother Gertrude, the person I had fought so hard to defend, had completely betrayed me.

Gertrude had deliberately and consciously separated me from the very people who loved me.

I felt she was afraid to tell me anything because she feared she would lose me if I knew the truth. This all began to make sense even though it was unsettling.

163

I reflected on all the times I had asked her about Sisi or my birth mother and she chose to lie. I wondered what this had done to her.

Being with Sisi was such a gift as she made me feel loved and less crazy. I now had some accurate information surrounding my adoption that could help me heal my heart. I still had many more questions, but our conversation ended as we needed to prepare for our visit to the home Sisi and I had lived in together fifty years before. I wondered what I would notice now that I was more aware. I was curious on so many levels to see where my father's office was and to see my bedroom where the Tree Spirit gave me my message. I was looking forward to walking into my mother's photo studio and standing on the stairs, imagining the moment I had floated down them as a child. This house was so special to me, and to be able to return with Sisi made it feel so right.

We boarded the U-Bahn, Frankfurt's tram system, and rode to 2 Fürstenburger Strasse. It was a beautiful spring day that was filled with anticipation. When we walked off the tram, I could immediately see the roofline of our home peering above the trees a block away. As we walked closer, I was again amazed by its sheer size and beauty. When we reached the front entrance, we swung open the green metal gate and walked into the courtyard. This was my home, and it, too, felt exactly as it did when I left.

Standing at the base of the house just took my breath away. This immense and enchanting ivy-covered villa filled my heart with flashes of memories of the childhood I longed to believe in.

The front steps led to a ground level window before turning right and continuing up to a massive wooden door.

Hazel greeted us at the front door but said her husband Rolph was not feeling well so only three people could come inside the home.

We quickly decided that Sisi and Sabine would accompany me. I was very sad that Paul, Tyler and Heinz were not going to share in this experience, but I had no choice and needed to respect their wishes.

Paul said he would take Tyler and Heinz to Holzhausen Park and wait for us until we were finished. I was so grateful for his graciousness because this was truly awkward and disappointing for all of us.

As they walked away, we walked up the steps and through the front door. It was like walking back in time. Other than the wall colors, it looked like the same house.

Hazel had set up a tea for the three of us with muffins, cookies, and candies. She and Rolph were both very gracious. They opened up the main floor for us to explore. I walked around with Sisi and Sabine as we shared memories of the living room, dining room, and kitchen. Then we walked into the vaulted library room with its huge double doors. This was the room that housed our eighteen-foot Christmas tree each year. I wished Tyler and Paul were with me to see this. My head was spinning trying to soak it all in.

We were led up the stairs to where our bedrooms were. I stood in my bedroom where I had received the Tree Spirit's message. It still held the energy of something or someone, but I couldn't explain it. Hazel told us that spirits lived in the house, but she didn't want to elaborate on it. Sisi showed me her room and Tanta's. She also pointed to the room where my father's CIA unit was housed. When she opened the door to his office, I saw a massive rectangular room. Three large windows offered an expansive view down Oeder Weg. What a great vantage point they had! This floor alone had six bedrooms and two bathrooms. We were standing on a well-worn wooden floor in a large open space surrounded by doors. This space held a lot of magic, which all began to flood back to me.

165

My eyes drifted up the massive open staircase to the sixth-floor balcony that now surrounded us from above. I wanted to go up to that level where Henry and I played, but we couldn't. Stacks of newspapers barricaded the front of the staircase. Clearly, we weren't allowed to go any higher. I could see lots of boxes and piles of stuff through the railings around the balcony. I realized we wouldn't be able to walk through it even if we tried. I was again disappointed, for this also meant that I wouldn't be able to see where my mother's photo lab used to be.

As a consolation we were invited to tour the three lower levels. Sisi and Sabine stayed behind. It was surprising that she had left all three of these floors totally empty. They looked exactly as they had when I was a child.

The entire garden floor level was completely intact. I could now see that this was originally the servants' quarters that had been turned into a makeshift hospital during the war. Everything had been painted white, but now it was a dingy shade of ivory. I found it absolutely enchanting. Light was streaming through all the small windows in each of the rooms throughout the floor. I walked over to the side entrance door and remembered myself as a little girl using this secret door to enter the home whenever I played outside on the swing.

We went down another set of stairs to the storage level below. It featured a large root cellar and a vaulted wine cellar, plus a secret entrance to the hidden bomb shelter.

I had never seen the bomb shelter and was intrigued by its construction. I could see that large boulders formed what felt more like a cave. Dark wooden beams supported the ceiling, and a tiny wooden shutter served as an airshaft that led up to the yard above us. I imagined people crouched together in this space as the bombs dropped in 1944.

As the history of the home came alive for me, I started coughing. The dust had triggered an asthma attack and I felt as if I was being suffocated. Everything in my body told me to get out of the house as fast as I could. As soon as I reached Sisi she could see the distress I was in.

We quickly said our goodbyes and walked out the front door to Holzhausen Park to find Paul, Tyler and Heinz. It had been a very intense visit but I was grateful to have had the chance to feel and see the house again.

Once we were all together again, Sisi and Heinz treated us to lunch at the Italian restaurant we used to go to when I was young. It was wonderful to share a meal together in a familiar place. After lunch Sisi and Heinz had to board the tram to their home in Wiesbaden. We all cried as we hugged each other good-bye. I wondered in my heart when (or if) I would see them again. Our time together was too short. Everything washed over me like a fog.

It was Easter weekend and Sisi had given us all some Easter chocolates. She gifted me a pair of porcelain penguins that represented her and Heinz. They also gave each of us an envelope with 50 euros in it to buy something as a remembrance of them. That weekend, Paul, Tyler and I went to a street fair along the Main River where I found a beautiful, pewter swan. I bought it to honor Sisi and the swans that used to swim in Holzhausen Park. Paul bought a leather backpack and Tyler found an acoustic guitar.

I had also brought all of my adoption papers with me so I could go to the City Hall (Standesampt). I was hoping to get more information about Henrietta and possibly my great-grandparents.

I soon discovered that during Easter, everything in Frankfurt basically shuts down for four full days. I had planned this trip carefully, but had not expected this.

I was disappointed, but I felt there must be a reason that I was not to know this now.

Fortunately, I had booked a one-day cruise along the Rhine River that same weekend. This gave me a chance to show Tyler and Paul the countryside I grew up with. Castles, vineyards and multi-colored fields created a patchwork quilt on both sides of the river. I was thrilled beyond belief to be here once again and to share this with Tyler and Paul. The boat stopped at a small restaurant and winery where we had a traditional German meal and bought some German Eiswein. On Easter Sunday we visited the Palmengarten, a 50-acre botanical garden in the heart Frankfurt. This was another one of my childhood memories, and it was within walking distance to Holzhausen Park.

The next day we flew to Paris and checked into our hotel near the Seine. We walked to Notre Dame, the Louvre and the Pantheon, as well as multiple parks and museums. We took a cab to the Eiffel Tower and the Pere Lachaise Cemetery. Tyler wanted to visit Jim Morrison's grave. Overall, the energy of Paris was intense and challenging. I was glad we booked a trip to the French countryside. We traveled to Giverny and toured Monet's Gardens. We went to the town of Auvers-sur-Oise, the last home of Vincent Van Gogh, where he and his brother Theo are buried.

Before returning to the United States, we spent a week in Amsterdam on the same street where Anne Frank had once lived and wrote her famous diary. Our hotel was just blocks from her secret annex on Prinsengracht Canal. Every day we could hear the same church bells that she wrote of. It was magical. Anne Frank's diary was the inspiration for journaling my own life and my feelings.

Journaling was like having a constant friend at my side. I could pour out my feelings, my dreams, and my fears onto those pages.

Interestingly, it was not until this trip that I realized Anne Frank was born in Frankfurt, just like me. I thought to myself what an odd coincidence that I was asked to play her in grade school. My connection with Anne grew even deeper when I learned of her love for a horse chestnut tree that stood outside the secret annex where she and her family hid. She wrote about it several times in her dairy. We walked over to the Anne Frank house to get a closer look and discovered that they were actually trying to save her 150-year-old horse chestnut tree from falling over. A disease had eaten away its core, and protective barriers were set up around it.

We did not go into the house itself because scaffolding surrounded it. I felt I was being protected from the sadness I would feel if I actually walked inside.

As I stood on the cobblestone sidewalk and looked up at the windows I sensed I had been here before. I connected with her tree from a distance and felt the sweetness of its shade and the strength of its branches. Anne didn't get to say goodbye to her tree, and I didn't get to say goodbye to mine either. It was an honor to stand witness for the last days of her tree's life and experience one of the many connections we shared.

In Amsterdam, we visited the famous Rijksmuseum and the Hortus Botanicus garden, and walked the charming streets within the city's inner Canal Ring. Each day brought a new discovery. On our last day we scheduled a trip to Keukenhof Gardens. It was April in Holland. This was the perfect time to see the gardens because all of the tulips were now in full bloom. As soon as we crossed the bridge into the gardens, I felt transformed. It was a Technicolor fairyland.

White trumpeter swans were swimming in crystal clear ponds surrounded by massive manicured meadows of color. We walked the entire 80-acre complex.

Sunlight kissed each flower with dappled sunlight shining through a canopy of gigantic shade trees. My soul felt as if I had just walked through a magical portal. A white peacock seemed to lead the way as we walked on cobblestone paths through gardens of art. The flowers looked like colors on a canvas that flowed throughout this magical wonderland. It felt like I was in a dream world, only I was totally awake.

In that moment I remembered the luminous egg I was carrying within me from my session with Michael back in Green Bay.

Out of the corner of my eye, I saw a group of people surrounding a table on the lawn ahead of us. I walked over to see what was going on and discovered an artist who was selling small ceramic animals.

That was when I saw a beautiful blue turtle with a baby turtle on its back!

"How much does the blue turtle cost?" I asked.

"Fourteen euros, cash only," she said.

I didn't have fourteen euros. I asked Paul and Tyler if they had any they could give me. Even though they thought I was a little crazy, they knew what the egg meant to me. They dug into their pockets until we had enough euros to purchase it!

As I held it in my hand, I could feel its magic. I felt that I was the baby turtle sitting on my mother's back while she was carrying me safely home.

CHAPTER 14 – THE START

In May 2007, I traveled to Madison, Wisconsin to begin the Four Winds Medicine Wheel program and the Healing the Light Body practitioner training.

This first week-long intensive (south direction) focused on shedding our pain stories, or original wounds, like a serpent sheds its skin. I focused on releasing my three primary wounds around anger, betrayal, and confusion.

I gave myself permission to shed the anger I had been holding. For the most part, I was able to control my anger-except when it would escape in brief yet frightening fits of pure rage. The anger I held within me was so raw that I never wanted to see it or feel it. Now I knew I had no choice but to look at it and hopefully let it go. I was angry with my parents for lying to me about coming to America and losing touch with Sisi and Heinz when they both knew how much I loved them. I was angry for being beaten up by my classmates and not feeling protected or validated. I was angry with Gertrude when she found my birth control pills and said I was a "bad seed." I was angry that she said she wished she had never adopted me, knowing that my mother Karin never wanted to let me go. I was angry with Gertrude for hiring a lawyer to force Karin into signing the papers and then telling me she was a no-good drunken prostitute. I was angry with both of my adoptive parents for denying me the chance of knowing my birth parents and their story. I allowed all of this anger to flow through me and into this stone that was placed on my stomach. It was as if my body said, "Enough!"

I found myself exhausted and at peace. It was a strangely sweet and serene feeling.

The second wound I wanted to shed was the betrayal I felt in my heart. As I breathed into this wound, I sensed I was falling into a bottomless hole located in my heart. The more I released, the deeper I fell. I began to panic. Eventually our teacher came in and stopped my session. She saw that this was a much bigger issue than what I could release right now. She said this was probably going to be my primary focus throughout my healing journey.

I moved on to focus on shedding the pain and confusion of being bullied and beaten as a child in Algoma. I used my breath to release the humiliation I felt. As I did, I sensed a large white swan spreading its wings over my torso. I imagined it was one of the white trumpeter swans I fed in Holzhausen Park. The embrace and love I felt from this energetic swan filled me with a sense of innocence and wonder. I thought of the fairy tale *The Ugly Duckling* and how it turned into a beautiful swan. I believed this swan was here to remind me of the beauty that was my childhood, and to help me release the pain.

By the end of the week, we had done three personal sessions on ourselves and exchanged six practice sessions with each other. This meant I had six opportunities to release a great deal of pain. I could now see that my issue of betrayal was intertwined with my anger and confusion like one big ball of knots, which I was excited to untangle.

A week later, I had a very vivid dream, where Paul and I were living in a small red room, but we had to move out. Then we were in a big house made of stone on a cliff next to an ocean. As I looked around the house, I found a basement with two rooms. One room was a totally intact nursery from the 1800s with old, wicker baby furniture. Paul walked into the other room, which was full of paint cans.

I was being asked to take a woman I barely knew to a New Age school for social work. The school's doors were small, so I had to duck down to get in. Inside were a group of young men trying to step on a swinging pine tree hanging upside down tied onto a rope. They were trying to stop it from swinging by stepping on the tip of the tree as it dragged across the floor. If they succeeded, they were allowed to swear or say whatever outlandish social commentary they wanted. I became outraged and started yelling at them to stop. The professor came over to me and asked what my problem was. I told him that it was cruel and insensitive to be treating a tree like that. I asked him why he was encouraging such horrible behavior. He brought me to the tree and said, "Look at it. It's dead, so it doesn't matter if they step on it or not."

I said, "It's not dead. It's hanging upside down."

I untied the tree so it could stand upright. Its branches opened up as it breathed a sigh of relief. Clearly the tree was very much alive.

The professor and the students were amazed and shocked. They said they were sorry and that if they had known the tree wasn't dead, they wouldn't have done it.

I said, "It's not a matter of whether the tree is dead or not. It's how you looked at it and disrespected it."

Then, all of a sudden, I found myself walking alone on a beach at night. The moonlight was casting a dim light so I could see where I was going. A voice yelled in my head, "Watch out, the eagle is going to get you and sweep you away and eat you, and you will be dead."

I looked to my right and saw the faint outline of mountains in the distance. To my left was an expansive ocean rolling in with the tide. I looked straight ahead and saw an endless stretch of sandy beach with no tracks. I looked to the night sky above me and didn't see an eagle.

As I continued walking, I noticed a row of pedestals on my right.

A series of large geometric crystals were perched on each one. The pedestals became taller as I walked along. The voice continued repeating its message, trying to scare me. I kept walking, looking to see where the voice was coming from but saw nothing. After I passed the 13th crystal, I saw a little light in the distance. I approached an open porch with stone steps. As I ascended the steps, I felt the eagle swoop up behind me – letting me know that he had my back the entire way. I looked up and saw Paul sitting in a wicker chair under the light of a single exposed bulb.

When I woke up, I felt that the eagle had guided me home where I was safe and could rest.

As I tried to interpret the dream, I realized that the house represented the separate paths Paul and I were on.

He had gone into the room filled with paint because it symbolized his desire to be an oil painter.

I passed by an old, abandoned nursery based on my childhood wounds.

The New Age social work school was my shamanic training, and the tree hanging upside down was me!

The walk on the beach was the journey I was now on, and the voice inside my head was trying to make me fear the work I was doing.

The eagle represented my ability to see beyond my fear and to see my life from a new perspective by honoring the wisdom growing within me.

To see Paul at the end of the dream was so comforting to me. Even though we may be on separate paths, I felt we would always come home to each other at the end of the day.

CHAPTER 15 – THE RELEASE

A few weeks after my first Four Winds training, I went to see a shamanic reiki healer. She sensed male energy and questioned me about my relationship with my father.

"Which one?" I responded.

"The father that is your birth father," she said.

"Oh, that would be Lonnie." I was puzzled and a little annoyed that he kept coming up in my sessions. I wanted to connect with my mother Karin and heal the loss I felt for her.

"So, what do you feel when you think of your birth father Lonnie?" she asked.

"I don't know him, we never met," I replied.

She asked me to close my eyes and begin imagining him in the room. As I did, I began to feel the presence of a large wolf pacing around a very old tree. I sensed Lonnie was the wolf and I was the tree. I watched the wolf slowly approach the twisted roots of the tree that were protruding from the ground. When it reached the base of the tree, the wolf became smaller and turned into a green lizard that crawled up the trunk and into a dark hole in the center. When the lizard disappeared, I felt my spirit being drawn through that same small dark hole. Before I knew it, I emerged through the top of the tree and was now on the ground. My mother Karin and my father Lonnie were encircling me with their hands held together. I was standing in the middle of the circle, feeling the love they had for me and each other.

I recalled Viola's words to me, "Mom wanted you to have this ring because it would be a reminder for you that you were born from the love of a mother and a father." I now felt how much they loved each other and me.

The next day, I woke up feeling as if Lonnie wanted me to connect with him visually in real time. I went to the computer and searched the internet for his name. After two hours of searching, I had nothing. Then I remembered the video I created thirteen years ago and put it into the VCR. I was shocked to see that the opening shot was of my father's portrait hanging in my mother's living room with the words: "Father's Day - June 19, 1994." Yesterday was June 19, 2007. Thirteen years had passed since that day. He was sending a clear message that he was with me, and he wanted me to know that what had happened yesterday was real.

As I accepted this message, I realized that the number thirteen was also very significant to me. Karin had died on my thirteenth wedding anniversary with Paul, which was the same day that I received her anniversary ring from Lonnie.

I decided to set up a healing altar for all of my parents: John and Gertrude, Lonnie and Karin. Even though they were not on this Earth, I felt their spirits were ready to begin making peace with each other, and I with them. I put photos of each of them on the altar. When I finished the altar, I began talking to them individually and out loud. I placed rose petals in front of their photos. I could feel the energy beginning to shift between all of us.

Altar for my parents. Gertrude, John, Karin, Lonnie.

It was now Saturday, July 7, 2007. (07/07/07). Yesterday was my last day as president of Infusion Inc.

I was moving forward knowing I had lost my investment in the agency along with any hope of supplemental income to help me pursue this new path. As hard as it was, I had to let it go.

Today was the "official" day that I wanted to honor this new path I was on with my closest friends. After dinner that evening, we gathered around a ceremonial fire in our backyard. It was beautiful and it meant a lot that they came to support me, even though some thought I was a little crazy.

When we walked back into the house it became clear that we had been robbed! Two of my friend's purses were missing and panic ensued. What began as a sacred evening turned into a nightmare! We called the police and reported what happened. The party ended in total chaos.

After everyone left, I sat outside and asked the Universe why. Why would you let this happen on a night like this; why tonight of all nights? All the anger, confusion and betrayal I had just released came roaring back. It was hard to accept, for I felt betrayed by the Universe.

I spent several days driving my friends around to renew and replace their SS cards, licenses etc. I was willing to do anything to help them restore what they had lost. I was grateful to have such remarkable and compassionate friends. Not everyone would have been as gracious as they were, especially since their purses were never found.

This experience forced me to see that my feeling betrayed was actually a choice I had to make. I needed to release my expectations of what "should be" and stop feeling like a powerless victim.

"The clearest way into the universe
is through a forest wilderness."
- John Muir -

CHAPTER 16 – THE WONDER

It was August 2007. I was driving a silver rental car up the steep, curvy dirt roads leading to the Mount Madonna Center in central California. This was a working ashram nestled among giant redwoods with spectacular vistas overlooking Monterey Bay. Mount Madonna was the home of Baba Hari Dass (Babaji), a silent yogi born in India.

I was looking forward to becoming more aware of the rich, spiritual ceremonies and traditions of India and Hinduism. It was enchanting waking to the sound of temple bells and the call of the conch shell every morning. Everyone who stays there is invited to the Sankat Mochan Hanuman Temple for Puja, a sacred Hindu ceremony that is performed several times a day in an outdoor temple.

I attended my first Puja on the second day. It was intoxicating to feel the beauty of this open-air temple and the ritual smell of sandalwood and candles. A young Hindu priest rang several brass bells and lit a lamp filled with camphor. He began to move the lamp in a circular motion around a sacred statue of the deity Hanuman. He offered flowers and candies (*prasad*) from a special tray and placed them onto the statue. We sang songs (*kirtan*) and were invited to come up and receive a blessing in the form of a red bindi dot placed on the middle of our forehead. This bindi dot signified the opening of our third eye, or inner knowing.

The retreat itself was a silent retreat called *"The Sacred Art of Awakening."* It was a five-day mandala retreat led by Dr. Judith Cornell. As soon as I arrived, I had to choose a word that replaced my actual name.

I chose the name Wonder.

179

It felt right to me, for I was wondering about a lot of things and hoping for some clarity.

Dr. Cornell took us through a guided meditation to open our heart's mind (third eye) and receive a healing symbol. As I went into meditation I felt my mind being pulled into my heart. As I connected with my heart, I began drawing a large tree without any leaves, as if it were winter. Light was radiating from a little hole in the middle of the trunk, shining in all directions. I felt safe within this tree, yet I could still shine light out for others. After we finished drawing the mandala we were asked to meditate on its meaning. What came through was both surprising and direct.

You are the wonder that shines out for the world. In your soul you now have the answers you seek. You are the tree rooted in the sweetness of Mother Earth yet reaching for the highest points in the universe. Through me you will find your soul, for I have been protecting it for you until you are ready to know the true beauty and light that shines within you. You see the world through me, you try to make sense of mankind in my branches, you want to hide in the safety of my caress, in the shadows I cast. But you cannot. I continue to grow just as you must, so leave my hiding place and step into your light. I will always be here for you and within you. You are a child of the everlasting seed of love and life. Go and share the wonder you hold with the world. And remember to reach out to me for I will be always be here to love you unconditionally.

Every day after that, we experienced poetry; readings, songs, dance etc. based on Islamic, Christian, Jewish, Hindu, and Buddhist teachings as well as earth-based beliefs.

I connected with how each belief had inspired me.

I drew seven mandalas inspired by each religion; being in silence encouraged deeper reflection.

A few days after I returned from California, I received an e-mail with a photo of the first mandala I had drawn. To my surprise, I could now see that it had the shape of a distinct "spirit" in the trunk of the tree.

My first mandala of the Tree Spirit.

The light I had drawn was radiating directly from the heart of this spirit. I could feel the positive shifts that were occurring within my heart. This was a powerful affirmation for me that I had made the right decision to leave my job.

As I reflected on the mandala, I noticed that I had drawn a large spider web around the entire image. This meant that I had much more work ahead of me if I wanted to clean out the cobwebs and understand my true roots.

*"Maybe you are searching among branches
for what only appears in the Roots."*
- Rumi -

CHAPTER 17: THE ROOTS

Everywhere I looked, I started to notice more and more synchronicities and little coincidences that seemed statistically unlikely yet were uncannily meaningful. These synchronicities were often associated with life events and sometimes appeared to me in the form of numbers.

Today was September 25, 2007, my father John's birthday. He had died 25 years ago on June 25, 1982. The number 25 jumped out at me again. $(2 + 5 = 7!)$

These numbers gave me comfort; this synchronicity reminded me that I missed him terribly and wished he were here to talk to about all that I was learning and feeling.

I decided to pull two animal cards, from Ted Andrews *Animal Speak Tarot;* One for my father John and one for me. I had been working with these cards for over six years and found them to be extremely helpful when I was in need of guidance or inspiration. The card I pulled for my father was the horse! My father John wanted to raise horses when he retired. Paul and I had placed his ashes in a horse pasture. Plus, the horse on the card was a palomino, his favorite horse. I placed the horse card in front of his photo on my altar and lit a candle to honor the love I felt for him.

A few days later, Paul came home with several pieces of petrified wood from the Chickaloon River Canyon in Alaska. He bought them from an elderly woman who had traveled to Alaska with a geology group. She told him that these stones were formed from trees that lived 55 million years ago when Alaska was a tropical rainforest.

One piece in particular reminded me of the tree spirit as well as the spirit that appeared in my first mandala.

As I held each piece, I could feel myself connecting with this ancient tree. I soon discovered that there were conifer trees, specifically redwoods, living along the same route that humans traveled when they entered the Americas.

I was now creating a *mesa*, or personal medicine bundle, based in the Andean tradition. I had purchased an authentic *mestana* cloth, which was hand-woven by a Peruvian weaver in the Andes. Each cloth is thoughtfully woven to tell a story. These cloths were used to carry babies, food and belongings. The medicine people of the Andes, known as *paqos*, use these cloths to carry their personal medicine. A *mesa* can include herbs and flowers, as well as objects and sacred stones called *khuyas*. In the Andean tradition *khuyas* contain the energetic medicine of the *paqo*. These sacred *khuyas* also hold the energy of the place it originated from, as well as the path it traveled. As we begin to work with stones, similar to a worry stone, we can release our worry. In this case it becomes empowered with our intention to heal our wound. It's like a touchstone that connects us to the wisdom and power we feel as we transform our wounded stories into healed and powerful stories. This wisdom encourages us to step into our self as a person of peaceful power. Each *khuya* carries a specific intention and insight as we deepen our connection with it.

This fascinated me, for I had been collecting stones all my life. Living in Algoma I naturally collected stones along the shores of Lake Michigan. Everywhere I went I was drawn to stones. I had bowls and bowls of them in my home simply because they made me feel good. Now it seemed they were going to help me heal and reconnect with my true self.

I attended my second Four Winds training (west direction) in Spring Green, Wisconsin.

It was fall and the trees were in full color as they accented the open prairies and rolling hills of the Wisconsin River valley. The West is the direction of the setting or dying sun and the energy of Jaguar. Here we explored the dark or hidden parts of ourselves in order to come into right relationship with our fears, shadows and personal power. We also focused on unwinding the wounds of three ancestors.

I knew I wanted to work with Gertrude and Karin, but it was difficult to choose between Henrietta or my fathers, John and Lonnie. Ultimately, I chose Lonnie because I wanted to connect with any remaining fears or uncertainties I had toward him.

I used the yellow stone I found in Holzhausen Park to connect with the energy of Karin. It was beautiful and gentle, yet strong and wise.

I chose a deep red carnelian stone from Lake Superior to work with my mother Gertrude and her inability to have children, and how that wound affected our life.

The third stone was black with a hint of white on the back of one side. It had a scar-like marking that looked like stitches on the other side. I felt this stone represented my father Lonnie and all the battles he had lived through. The blackness carried the energy of mystery. The little white area carried the glimmer of hope within the darkness.

I partnered with a very wise and gracious woman who worked with me as I stepped into the role of each of my parents and then back into myself. By doing this, I was able to become them and ask the questions I had always wanted answered. I began feeling the struggles they faced as I tried to understand life from their perspective. Doing this helped me to appreciate the lessons and gifts they gave me.

185

We also worked on releasing memories held within our body that prevented us from moving forward. I knew that I was still holding onto the energy surrounding betrayal. I did not know where it all came from; all I knew was that I was so tired of hanging onto this and was more than ready to let it go. As I was lying on the floor, I began feeling a dark damp sensation inside of me. I became agitated when I felt my heart being invaded by the freezing cold again. This cold sensation in my heart was getting very old. As I connected with it, it felt as if my heart were encased in ice.

I immediately imagined a black, stone-like structure under my back, similar to a Mayan or Egyptian pyramid. I arched my back off the ground and slammed it over this imaginary pyramid to release my heart from this icy prison. I kept slamming my back onto the floor harder and harder until I felt the frozen energy disperse into a million pieces. The relief I felt was so overwhelming, I began sobbing.

"Laural, go to your source," my partner said.

I sensed a luminous, purple-blue thread shoot straight from my heart into the Universe. Tears were rolling down my cheeks as my body relaxed. By now several of my classmates were kneeling around me. They were shocked by the icy cold energy that was pouring off my hands. I then began feeling electricity in my hands; they were buzzing intensely. At this point our teacher reassured me that I had just released a huge energetic block from my body. I turned my hands down onto the floor beside me and felt my body reconnect with the Earth, as if I were being held and nurtured like an infant cradled in its mother's arms. I stayed on the floor for a long time, feeling held by pure love.

When I came home, I worked with a fourth stone that connected me to my father John. It was a small geode with blue crystals from Lake Michigan. I felt that it represented the all secrets he held, as well as his gentle nature.

I did not choose a stone for Henrietta. I was content, for now, to connect with my four immediate parents. I felt I needed to work with them before I could even think of dealing with what Henrietta represented.

Two days after this class, I awoke from a dream of my adoptive parents, Gertrude and John. In the dream, my mother was working really hard in my garden, trying to make things right between us. I remember wanting to go outside and make her come into the house to rest, but my father touched my arm and said, "No, Laural, she needs to do this for you and for herself."

I woke up feeling really at peace with my parents; it was very sweet, beautiful and real. I felt that Gertrude was telling me that she messed up my garden by disturbing my roots. Her desire to make things "right" - gave me the sense that she was letting me know that I was not a "bad seed." This made me wonder about my true biological "seed."

I decided to dig into my father Lonnie's roots with the help of ancestry.com. I learned that his ancestors were a mix of Scottish, English, Irish and German farmers who immigrated to the colonies between 1600 and 1750. They eventually moved onto Cherokee land in the Carolina's and Georgia. I discovered that several of my father's forefathers had fought in the Revolutionary War and the War of 1812. I learned that my great great grandfather was a member of Buffington's militia during the removal of the Cherokee in Georgia and later in life fought in the Civil War as a confederate soldier. My father Lonnie served in the army during WWII, Korea and Vietnam. His father fought in WWI. It seemed I came from a lineage of soldiers.

I began thinking of the stories Viola shared with me about our father and the secret fires he had in their backyard.

Apparently, Lonnie stood over the fires and quietly burned little black books until their contents were completely destroyed.

One day I received a surprise package in the mail. When I opened it, I was shocked to see that it held a little black book from my father and several undeveloped canisters of film. A letter inside explained that it was from Viola and how she had found this book and film in a box tucked away on the top shelf in our mother's closet. As I held the little black book in my hands and turned the pages, I was mesmerized to discover that he had scribbled drawings of star constellations, math formulas and sequential numbers in code, and the word hemlock. My father obviously knew how to track on several different levels. I'm sure some of this was his military training, but I also sensed it might have been instinctual. As I held his book, I sensed him guiding me.

We had decided to visit Tyler for the Holidays, while he was back in Asheville N.C. I asked Paul and Tyler if they wanted to drive to the Smoky Mountains on the Winter

Solstice to do a ceremony to honor my father's ancestors and to heal their wounds. As we drove through the tree lined-mountains I wondered what their lives were like. I imagined little log cabins carved in the forests. When we reached the highest point, I asked Paul to stop the car. I knew this was exactly where I needed to be. I called in the directions and invited the spirits of the land and my ancestors to join me.

Laural, in the Smoky Mountains on the Winter Solstice - 2007.

I looked at the misty, blue valley below and the endless waves of mountains beyond. I did a little ceremony to thank my ancestors for giving me life. I also prayed for the Cherokee and their land as well as those who were taken from their land in Africa and enslaved. I asked for healing for myself and those yet to come. When I finished, I thanked the directions for being my sacred witnesses. I felt connected to this land in a way that was hard to describe. It was home.

Afterwards we walked on a small trail along a nearby stream. It had rained just before we arrived and rainwater was trickling down the path. A small stone rolled to a stop at my foot. Intrigued, I bent down to pick it up. As I held it in my hands, it split in half revealing a fossilized impression of a leaf on both sides. It was dark grey and the texture felt like bark. I marveled at the "tree-like" image within the stone. It was the perfect stone for me to work with as it reminded me to understand and honor both sides of every story.

After our trip to Asheville, I began to dig into my mother Karin's ancestral lineage. Karin had given me photos of Henrietta's parents and grandparents. My great grandfather served in WWI, and his father served in the Prussian Imperial Army. It wasn't difficult for me to imagine that I had a "warrior" gene, but my goal was to bring peace.

I decided to do a mitochondrial DNA test, to see what else I inherited. I discovered that women can only trace their female lineage; meaning our mothers' mothers' lineage. Male ancestry is not recorded.

I sent for the test and within two weeks I had answers. I belonged to Haplogroup K which meant there was a probability of having Ashkenazi Jewish ancestry. Haplogroup K gets its name from "Katrine," who is identified as one of the seven founding daughters of "Eve."

The term Ashkenazi literally means "Jews of the Rhineland." I was intrigued by this result. My mother Karin had been told, after the war was over, that she had Jewish blood because her father's mother was a Sephardic Jew "Spanish Jew." This made me wonder if it was possible that my maternal lineage might have Ashkenazi Jewish blood. If so, it might be another reason why Henrietta joined the Nazi Party. Maybe she suspected that she might actually have Jewish ancestry, and she couldn't take any chances, especially since she had married a Jewish man. She may have felt she had no choice but to join so she could protect herself, her daughter Karin, as well as her parents. After all, Henrietta was their only child. My mind was racing imagining all of the possibilities. I tried to put it together, but finding names and identities of who was Jewish and who wasn't was nearly impossible, especially since so many Jews had converted to Christianity to survive by the 1800s.

I searched for records to see if Henrietta's name would show up, but I kept hitting wall after wall. I tried to find records of my maternal grandfather, but found nothing. It was frustrating to have so many dead ends and roadblocks. I wanted to understand what really happened to them and what the circumstances were that impacted their decisions.

I returned to Mount Madonna in February 2008 for my first mandala facilitator training. We had to set a personal intention before we began. My intention was to heal my Judeo-Christian roots.

Even though I wasn't a practicing Christian, I felt a strong connection to Jesus, a man born with Jewish blood. I was angry with the Church for distorting his teachings and instilling fear as a way to "convert" people to Christianity. I felt the Church had deliberately disconnected people from nature as a way to physically disempower them.

As I meditated, I saw an image of a cross and a tree. When I finished drawing, I instinctively began drawing blood pouring onto the roots of the tree. I was overcome with emotion for I felt the sadness, confusion and betrayal that the Church had created and how the cross had been used as a tool that separated people from each other. As I continued drawing, I began to feel that the tree was cleansing itself with the blood of our ancestors. When I stopped drawing blood, I felt the presence of a small white dove flying toward the east. As I drew it, I sensed it was a symbol of a new beginning.

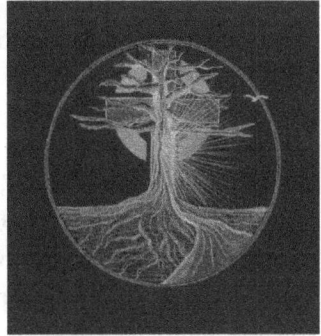

The Tree of Life healing the wounds of Christianity – a healing mandala.

When I shared my mandala with the class, I was stunned to learn that several other women had drawn similar images and were feeling much the same way as I was.

We cried together and released years of sadness and pain over this shared wound. We spontaneously and silently walked outside and held hands in a circle on the terrace. As we looked over the Pacific Ocean, one of the women in our group, a Christian Eastern Indian, sang the Lord's Prayer in Aramaic, the native tongue of Jesus. It was one of the most spiritual, sacred, and beautiful moments in my life. I felt that this mandala helped to heal years of confusion, fear and secrecy for generations before us and those yet to come.

During my second mandala meditation I found myself drawing the Star of David floating above an Egyptian desert. The star contained all the colors of the rainbow with the color red flowing into a large drop of blood suspended above a row of seven purple pyramids.

191

This mandala did not make me cry; it made me think. I wondered why I was able to allow the blood to flow so freely in the first mandala yet in this one I seemed to be holding onto it.

Curiously I had been shedding my own blood for the past four months. I wasn't overly concerned. I felt it was a natural part of perimenopause

Mandala holding a drop of blood.

and the fact that I was intentionally cleansing my ancestral roots.

When I returned home, I told a close friend that I had been bleeding since the beginning of November. She convinced me to see my doctor right away. My doctor immediately ordered an ultrasound and uterine biopsy. It was not a pleasant experience. I told my doctor that I felt this was an energetic cleanse; she looked at me like I was crazy. To everyone's surprise, all of the tests came back 100% normal, except for the fact that I was very anemic and still bleeding. It was now March. My doctor told me that it was time for me to stop the bleeding.

I wanted a ceremonial fire to help me finally release the ancestral wounds I was cleansing. I chose Maundy Thursday – the night that is symbolically associated with the Last Supper. I found it fitting as the body and blood of Christ is seen as the spiritual food that nurtures and sustains grace. I created a small *despacho*, an Andean prayer bundle, out of black construction paper. I drew a mandala with a cross, a star and a tree surrounded by an awakening spiral.

I wrote a note to the Universe asking to heal my ancestors and all that they may have harmed. I placed a small amount of my own menstrual blood into the *despacho* before folding it into a small square packet. I tied white cotton string around it and slid an Easter lily through the knot. I gently placed it into the fire and prayed for my ancestors and myself. I prayed for everyone who had been torn from their ancestral land and the families they left behind. I prayed for those who had been persecuted by religious zealots. I prayed for the victims of the Holocaust as well as the people of Germany. I prayed for everyone who held trauma in their genes. I prayed that the wounds of my ancestors would be released and replaced by wisdom and insight that could now be passed on to my son Tyler and his children.

After five months of continual bleeding, it stopped the following morning on Good Friday. I was amazed but not surprised. How perfect that it came full circle on Good Friday and the Spring Equinox - a time of renewal and birth.

"May life be like a great hospitable tree,
and may weary wanderers find in me a rest."
- John Henry Jowett -

CHAPTER 18: THE INSIGHTS

In May, 2008 I returned to Spring Green, for my third Four Winds training program (north direction). North represents the mythic and the energy of hummingbirds. This is where we learn about soul retrieval, which is what drew me into this work to begin with. I was excited to dive in.

We began by staging re-enactments of our soul loss stories through the use of role-playing. In my case two people from class stepped into the roles of my adoptive parents, Gertrude and John. They sat in front of me pretending to cradle an infant girl. They acted out the anguish of Gertrude and John as they refused to give me back to my birth mother. They had fallen in love with me and were determined to keep me even though Karin was also fighting to keep me. I had to step into their roles and feel the energy of what they were feeling. When I did, my heart heard John and Gertrude say, "We would rather die than have you know the truth about your adoption. If you knew the truth, you would not love us any longer, and we could not live with that pain." I sobbed at this discovery; it felt so true! My parents had hung onto this secret out of fear that I would hate them for what they did to my mother Karin. Instead, they chose to take my secret to their grave versus telling me the truth. I connected back to being myself and told them, "I will always love you, no matter what; even with everything I know. I understand why you felt you couldn't tell me and I forgive you. I know you loved me too much to give me back and were afraid I would love Karin more than you. I would have still loved you both even if you had told me the truth, for you are my parents and I know you did the best you could for me. I miss you both terribly and wish you were here."

It was a powerful process to have this opportunity to speak these words out loud as if John and Gertrude were in the room with me.

I traveled to Park City, Utah the following week to complete two of my three master classes in order to graduate. I had also been offering free personal sessions to my friends based on tools I now felt comfortable with.

The first class, *Walking with Protection*, was focused on the fact that fear is our biggest enemy. By tracking our fear, we become more conscious of it so we can learn from it and release what holds us. At the end of the week, we broke into small groups and discussed the issues we tracked. When it was my turn, one of the women in my group sensed I was holding onto an energy that had been guiding me and supporting me, but that I needed to release it in order to stand on my own. I silently wondered if it was my Tree Spirit. I knew that a big part of my healing journey was to trust and let go, which was interesting, considering that my biggest wound centered on feelings of being betrayed and abandoned. I allowed myself to release my fear of being alone. By facing this fear head on, I was no longer held by it even though I was very aware of it.

The second week was *Working with the Sacred*. Here look at our life as if it were a sacred fairy tale. By doing this, we are able to step out of our personal story and into a more imaginary story without the boundaries of time and space. Looking at life from this perspective allows us to see how our personal wounds are also held within the collective unconscious. From this place we can begin to rewrite them. Both the Four Winds and Judith Cornell embraced the word of Carl Jung, a Swiss psychologist.

Jung believed that to heal the psyche required a journey within where the self and soul could reconnect. By awakening our unconscious self, we become conscious of ourself as a soul. By becoming conscious of our soul, we can tap into the collective unconsciousness and begin to heal our wounded stories on an archetypal or sacred level.

I reflected on the mandalas I was creating and my fascination with trees. I was thrilled to learn that Carl Jung saw trees as the archetype of the psyche and that he felt mandalas were the archetype of wholeness.

Later that same summer I returned to Utah for my final master's class, *Reading the Signs of Destiny.* Here we learned the art of owning our intuitive gifts by learning various methods of divination. At the end of the class, we were asked to step into an alter ego and participate in a "psycho-psychic" fair. Everyone was invited to set up a booth where they could demonstrate their "gifts".

Upon hearing the word "psychic," the thing that came to mind was my mother Karin asking me on the phone if I was psychic and me saying yes. How thrilled she was to know that I had this gift! At the same time, I thought of Gertrude and how disturbed she was whenever I would mention anything about being psychic or spiritual. What a contrast this word represented for me.

As I thought about which alter ego I should step into, it came to me – in complete clarity: Step into who I truly am, step into Carmen Sylvia, and claim myself as the Tree Spirit by calling myself a Tree Oracle. It's time to step into my true birthright! It all seemed so simple and yet so profound.

By taking on the identity of a Tree Oracle, I was honoring the Tree Spirit within by connecting with my ancestral roots and my eternal soul at the same time.

By taking on my true identity as Carmen Sylvia, I was finally claiming the fact that this name was given to me with love and intention. I felt alive as I imagined being reborn as my authentic self. All the years of wondering where I came from began to dissipate. I prepared for the fair by creating a small sign with my signature on it. As I wrote my name "Carmen Sylvia" in cursive, I felt the enormity of what this meant. With every stroke, my heart expanded as I stepped into my truth. I realized from the depths of my being that I had chosen this life, as well as each of my parents.

I thought of my mother Gertrude and my father John and how connected I was to them. My soul had chosen them to be my parents so they could teach me what I needed to learn. It wasn't an accident that they raised me. It was a gift.

I thought of my mother, Karin, and how I had chosen her to be my birth mother. Our connection to each other was such an affirmation. She helped me on a soul level.

I thought of my father Lonnie and how I had chosen him to be my invisible father and hone my tracking skills. He encouraged me to search deeper and overcome my fears.

I remembered my grandfather Virtues and his story of my great grandfather who claimed the surname Virtues that guided and inspired me throughout my life.

I reflected on my grandmother Henrietta. I thought of all the secrets she held and how she had tried to fix the horrible mistakes she made before she died.

I also began to wonder if it was an aspect of my soul that appeared to me in the tree before my world flipped upside down, so I would remember who I truly was.

CHAPTER 19 – FULL CIRCLE

It was late fall when I attended my final intensive with the Four Winds (east direction) and the Healing the Light Body Training. This is the place of the rising sun and the energy of Eagle. This was a class of release and rebirth.

The timing was perfect, the trees outside my hotel window were releasing their leaves in the brisk wind of a cold November day. As they flew past my window, I was writing my life review on paper, in preparation for the sacred death that awaited me. Even though this wasn't a physical death, it was an energetic death that was symbolic of dying to my old stories and rebirthing myself, just as the sun does each morning. Through sacred drama and role-playing we created our own deathbed scenes.

This was a powerful process that involved choosing members of our class to play the roles of the most important people in our lives. I chose to have Paul and Tyler, along with all four of my parents. It was intense as I could truly feel them with me. Each person in my group took on the role assigned to them. I was laying on the floor covered in white sheets as if I were on my death bed, waiting for them to arrive. One by one, as they entered the space, they were transformed into my family member who was coming to me one last time. When Paul and Tyler came near, I reached out my hands and said, "I love you more than words can possibly express." I asked them to stay, as my parents began to gather around me one by one.

I introduced them one at a time to Paul and to Tyler, their grandson. Neither of my fathers had met Tyler, nor had he met them. Tyler had barely known his grandmothers.

It was important to me that they were connected on a soul level before I was gone. I wanted my parents to know their grandson and that he carried the family story that we had healed. I let them each know how much I loved them and what gifts they gave to me. I felt a sense of quiet tension in the room. I asked my parents to make peace with each other and to let me go, knowing that I loved them all equally. I had everyone hold hands above my heart and feel the love and connection we all shared. At that moment, I felt a beam shoot from my heart into their hands and out to the Universe. I could literally see a grid-like matrix all around me. The light that was emanating from their hands lit the grid that surrounded us all. I felt an enormous sense of peace and wholeness. I knew I was now ready. I imagined taking my last breath as the white sheet was gently pulled over my face. As I rested under the sheet, I felt my breath release any remaining sadness from my soul as my physical body stayed. When the group removed the sheet and welcomed me back, I felt reborn, as if a huge weight had been lifted off of me.

Later that night we had our graduation ceremony. I stepped forward and announced, "I am Laural Virtues Wauters, born Carmen Sylvia, and I proudly reclaim my roots!" My feet felt firmly planted in the earth and my arms were reaching to the sky like branches. I held my *mesa* above my head and felt like the Tree of Life itself.

Soon after my return, I went to see my doctor for my annual physical. When she came into the exam room, she couldn't believe how much younger I looked.

It became obvious to her that I had indeed shifted my physical body over the past year. I had lost weight, my blood pressure was 114/72, my cholesterol was good.

I had taken myself off of all asthma medications and had not had an asthma attack in over a year. I hadn't had any migraine headaches and my night terrors had stopped, plus I had been sleeping through the night. When she listened to my heart, she was shocked to hear that my heart murmur was gone! She asked me what I had been doing to bring about such a dramatic change. I told her I had shifted my reality; it had nothing to do with diet or exercise. She seemed to be intrigued by what she saw and asked me if I thought I could help others. I said yes. It was so validating to realize just how far I had come, not only emotionally but physically.

The time had come for me to travel back to Mount Madonna to finish my mandala facilitator training. I had completed my 108 hours of mandala facilitation by offering mandala classes at a local yoga studio and other venues.

This trip was bittersweet, as it happened to fall on January 30, Paul's and my wedding anniversary.

The only other time we had been apart on this day was when my mother Karin died 14 years ago. It was on that day that I was gifted her anniversary ring with the seven diamonds. As I glanced at it on my right hand, I reflected on the wedding ring from Paul on my left.

By now I understood the significance and synchronicity of this date. Hitler took power on January 30, 1933, the same year my mother Karin was born. Paul and I were married on January 30, 1982. My mother Karin died on January 30, 1995. Now, I was becoming a mandala facilitator on January 30, 2009.

I felt my life had come full-circle.

That evening I created a mandala based on an intention card. I pulled "Loving unconditionally with no strings attached."

I felt this was perfect as I began to create a mandala filled with love and gratitude. After it was finished, we were told to place them into a ceremonial fire to practice non-attachment. I was conflicted about releasing the concept of loving unconditionally, but I trusted the process.

The next morning while taking a shower, I felt that half of my wedding ring had completely broken off. All that was left was the bottom half of the ring soldered onto my anniversary ring. The entire setting with my mother Gertrude's diamond was gone! I panicked. I began to retrace my steps from the night before, looking for the top half of the ring. At the same time, I realized I had to accept it.

I knew this was related to the lesson of non-attachment. Once that realization became clear, I relaxed and went to my room. As I was choosing what to wear, I heard a thud on the carpet below. There was the missing portion of my ring with Gertrude's diamond firmly in place. I picked it up and put the two pieces into a little mesh bag and carried it with me for the rest of the day.

As the day went on, I understood that this was a message from Gertrude. She wanted me to know that she too loved me unconditionally with no strings attached.

Soon after I returned from California, I began smelling lilies wherever I went, yet there were none around. How could I smell something that wasn't there? My mind flashed to the despacho with the white lily in the fire. I looked at the calendar to verify the date and there it was.

Today was March 20, 2009 - exactly one year after I released the wounds of my ancestors and asked the bleeding to stop. I felt the lilies were reminding me of this shift and to acknowledge that I was now reclaiming my true self.

I no longer felt like a "bad seed." I had transformed from the wounded child into a wise woman.

A few days later, a friend told me that my name Carmen was Hebrew for "guardian" and Sylvia was German for "tree or forest." I was stunned! My mother, Karin, had given me a name that actually meant "Guardian Tree."

I felt compelled to better understand the name Gertrude and John had given me. Laural is commonly spelled Laurel, from the Latin word "*laurus*" for laurel trees. Bay laurel leaves were used in Greco-Roman times as a wreath or crown, to represent nobility, truth, and honor. Virtues comes from the Latin word "*virtus*," meaning moral excellence. Combined my name, Laural Virtues, means the "The Noble Trees of Moral Excellence."

This was truly fascinating that both of my names were associated with trees. My soul had made itself so obvious that there was no way I could deny that my Tree Spirit was and would always be a part of who I am!

Paul and I had planned another trip to Oregon in late August to visit Tyler. This time I was feeling drawn to visit Mount Shasta in northern California.

As I prepared for our trip, I learned that it had been a very sacred mountain for thousands of years. The native people that had lived there felt that it was a sacred place that connected them to Father Sky. I wanted to feel the energy of this sacred mountain and the community that was created around it. As we drove south, a turn on the interstate revealed a lone, snow-covered mountain in the distance.

My heart began to leap. Mount Shasta felt so familiar to me, yet I had never been there before. I felt I was seeing the Alps of my childhood. Eventually, we were driving up a winding road near the top of the mountain. A parking lot marked the end of the road. From there, we could hike up as far as we wanted.

Mount Shasta at this point was very arid; there were only a few individual pine trees scattered around the barren stone and dirt surface. A large, flat stone invited me to lie on it. I felt its warmth on my back as if the stone were cradling me in preparation for the journey ahead. Once I felt ready, I sat up and looked around.

I felt drawn to one particular tree perched next to a large boulder about 200 yards in front of me. When I reached that destination, I sat on a ledge of the boulder. I thanked the tree for its shade and silently asked the Universe, "Why am I here?" At that exact moment, my watch fell off my wrist and onto the ground. I looked at it lying next to my feet and wondered how it had unclasped itself. My watch had never fallen off before.

I was stunned when I saw that the time was 7:00! The number seven carried great significance for me.

I felt it was an affirmation that I was on the right path. My final day at the agency had been 7/7/7. The number seven had been guiding me throughout this journey.

This was a message from the Universe asking me to stop for a while and breathe. I reached down to pick up my watch from the dry, dusty earth beneath my feet. I held it in my hand and felt the coldness of the metal and realized that it was time for me to stop wearing it.

As I lifted my head, the view in front of me was breathtaking. The sun was just beginning to set. The sky seemed to be taking on an otherworldly feeling as dusk settled in and around me.

I turned around and saw a large layout of stones that spelled out the words "I Am." I smiled and thanked the Universe for bringing me here to experience this amazing day. I felt my soul fully open to the fact that I was the one I had been looking for.

We walked down the mountain to our car and noticed a Peruvian family carrying chairs and blankets up the trail. I asked where they were going. They replied, "We are here to spend the night and look at the stars upside down." What a fascinating insight as life seemed to be flipping over in real time.

As we drove down the road of Mt. Shasta, another mountain rose in front of us. It reminded me of the pyramid I had imagined that helped me break up the ice around my heart over a year ago. I asked Paul to pull over so I could take it all in. When I stepped out of the car, I felt a warm gentle breeze caress my face. I felt my body fill with light, as the sun transitioned into a golden circle settling in for a long night's sleep.

Mount Shasta, California - 2009

This was the ultimate love story, when Father Sky kisses Mother Earth goodnight.

"I was seeing in a sacred manner
the shape of all things in the Spirit,
and the Shape of all Shapes
as they must live together like one being
and I saw that the sacred hoop of my people
was one of many hoops that made one circle,
wide as daylight and as starlight,
and in the center grew one mighty flowering tree
to shelter all the children of one mother and one father.
And I saw that it was holy."
- Black Elk -

CHAPTER 20 – MY AWAKENING

By now I had come to accept that I would never again see the actual tree that spoke to my soul 50 years ago.

I was now teaching a yearlong medicine wheel class along with mandala classes and doing personal sessions.

I mentioned Holzhausen Park to a young friend of mine during a session. A few weeks later, she surprised me with a print of an 1860 oil painting by Hans Thoma that her mother had found online. I carefully unrolled the sturdy paper until the full image was revealed.

I instantly recognized the beloved park of my childhood, captured in time exactly 100 years ago.

It was fascinating to see how it was surrounded by farmland, and that Frankfurt had not yet grown beyond the original fortress walls just a few blocks away.

My initial instinct was to frame it, so I did. When I returned home, I went online to search for an image of the painting to post on my facebook page.

Within minutes, another friend commented on my post with the question, "So, Laural, where is your tree?"

As soon as the question was asked, I saw it clearly in front of me. I sat there in total disbelief. I responded that it was the large tree behind the castle on the right.

When Paul came home from work I asked him to look at the painting. I wanted to see if he could remember where we had stood in the park five years earlier, sensing where the tree might have been.

"It's right there," he said, as he pointed to the tree.

I was so excited I could hardly contain myself.

Here it was in front of me like a family portrait. I reflected on how many years I had dreamt of seeing it again.

Hans Thoma painting of Holzhausen Estate - 1860

I soon found myself researching how long sweet chestnuts and oak trees could live. I learned that they could grow to be over a thousand years old! So yes, it was completely feasible that this grand old tree in the painting would still be standing in 1961.

I began searching for other images of the original Holzhausen Estate and discovered that in 1398 it was called the "desolation" or deserted land. This was the year that Johann von Holzhausen had acquired it. His son Hammen built the original garden estate in the early 1400s. I found an old blueprint of the landscaping plan and saw that this particular tree may have been planted around 1430.

I began to ask myself, "What else is right in front of me that I am not giving myself permission to see?" Within that moment, I felt a tidal wave of love and longing flood through me as my heart whispered the name, "Sisi." I froze as I realized that she was the only person still living on this Earth who had loved me since I was an infant.

How could I not see this? I reflected on our short visit over five years ago and knew in that instant that I needed to go back to Germany as soon as I possibly could. By now my heart was pounding with anticipation, as I felt alive inside in a way I had not felt in a really long time. This was another chance to love and be loved.

Since I had seen them last, I had gone through knee replacement surgery on my right knee the year before. I had been dealing with arthritis for quite a while, but it had become unbearable. I felt strong and confident in my ability to walk around but I wanted to look over the maps of Frankfurt just in case I needed backup. I went to the bookshelf to gather up the guide books when I noticed an old leatherbound book.

I pulled it from the shelf and saw that it was an 1849 edition of Faust – written by Johann Wolfgang von Goethe. I was fascinated because I didn't recall this book from my childhood. I faintly remembered that after Gertrude passed my brother Henry had dropped off a box of old books from her bookcase. I assumed this came from her. I opened it and saw the name Werner Hammerschmitt. I had no idea who that was. The book was written entirely in German, and someone must have loved it at some point because phrases were underlined and pencil drawings were scrawled in the margins. Curious, I researched a bit about Faust and learned that it was a story about an alchemist who sold his soul to the devil in exchange for knowledge and power.

I was fascinated, but put it back on the shelf.

It was fall of 2012, and Sisi and Heinz were now in their eighties. They owned an apartment in Wiesbaden, but didn't travel much. I knew I would need to visit them at their home, which was exciting for me as well.

I tried to contact Hazel but no one answered the phone; it just rang and rang. I had learned that her husband Dr. Rolf Rudiger-Stroth had passed away and I sensed Hazel was not well. I planned to go to the house when I was there to see if anyone would answer.

I contacted Sabine to see if she was available to translate. She had just moved to Frankfurt and was working for a large marketing firm downtown. She was excited to see Sisi, as well as Heinz and me. They had stayed in touch over the past five years, as Sabine had become an adopted granddaughter of sorts. This felt more and more like I was coming home to yet another family.

I decided to stay at the same hotel in Frankfurt that we had stayed in as a family, five years earlier. I chose to go alone. I wanted to immerse myself for ten days and feel what it meant to live in Frankfurt. I could barely contain the excitement that was bubbling up within me.

When I thought of how fast and hectic those few precious hours had been with Sisi five years ago, I knew we both deserved so much more.

CHAPTER 21 – COMING HOME

It was a beautiful fall day in October when I arrived in Frankfurt. As soon as I got settled, I walked to Holzhausen Park and my childhood home.

The piercing sound of a jackhammer broke through the silence of the surrounding neighborhood as a home was being remodeled near the park. Eventually it stopped and I could hear the muffled sounds of children playing in the park and trees rustling in the air.

I walked to the house on 2 Fürstenberger Str. but no one was there. It looked vacant and unkempt. I knocked on the gate and left a letter in the mailbox, hoping someone would find it and contact me. No one did.

As I entered the park, I felt my feet wobble slightly on the uneven cobblestone. A young couple passed by in deep conversation. I silently said hello to the trees, shrubs and stones and noticed that the park seemed a little tired and weary. I went to the spot where the tree had once stood, the ground still barren and flat. A thick hedge of thorny bushes stopped me from getting any closer.

I looked around and saw an open space that seemed to be inviting me to sit down. I walked over and found that it was covered with freshly fallen maple leaves. They were gigantic and had turned a stunning shade of golden yellow, creating a soft blanket upon the ground for me to enjoy.

For over an hour I sat there, taking in the energy of the space. I opened my mesa and silently shared my stories and stones with the park. A large oak seemed particularly interested, as if it were standing there watching me.

I was beginning to feel my childlike innocence awakening within me. I thanked the park for holding my soul as I closed my mesa. It was time for me to meet Sabine back at the hotel. I was excited to see her again and plan out our adventure.

As we walked into the restaurant, I noticed that the sign next door said Café Karin. I instantly imagined that this was the café where my mother Karin fell in love with my father Lonnie. I confided to Sabine about my secret desire to believe that the café next door was where my parents had fallen in love. After dinner, we went into Café Karin for coffee and torte. I noticed that Goethe's house was nearby.

The following morning, Sisi met us with hugs and tears of joy. As we sat in their living room, I noticed that the only family photos she had out were the ones I gave her.

Her living room was filled with an eclectic mix of Asian and Bavarian artifacts with mid-century modern furniture. A large blue Persian rug lay beneath my feet as we sat on a soft sofa near the window. Her house was immaculate and I felt immediately at home.

Sisi asked, "Why didn't Mrs. Virtues respond to my letters? I wrote several letters a year, every year since you left." She was still clearly upset. I could see the confusion and pain on her face and she desperately wanted to understand why.

I replied, "Sisi, I don't think my mother Gertrude understood the real reason why they left Germany until we moved to Algoma. I think the reason she stopped writing to you was because she was afraid that if you talked to me or wrote to me that I would ask you questions about who my real mother was and that you would tell me the truth."

As Sabine translated, I could see Sisi finally accepting what had happened and why.

212

Then Sisi looked at me and asked, "Did you ever ask about me? Did you ever want to know where I was?"

I began to cry as I saw the heartbreak in her eyes.

"Yes," I replied. "I asked for you all the time and my parents wouldn't tell me. Even when I was in college, I asked about you."

"I wanted to write to you but they said they didn't have your address." I went on to explain, "When I was a young girl I even wondered if maybe you and Heinz were my real parents and I began to think that was why my mother wouldn't tell me where you were."

I could see how bittersweet this news was for her to hear from me. She began tearing up as she clutched her chest. I could feel her heart breaking as she grieved for all the years we had lost together.

She began to tell me more about my parents Gertrude and John and what it was like to live there. It felt like she was opening up a chest filled with secrets she had sworn to protect out of loyalty to two people she greatly admired. But now, she too felt betrayed.

Sisi told me that my father John had over 100 agents that reported to him and how they would come to our house to turn in film and paperwork. She explained that I was forbidden to learn German as a child and that she, Tanta and Heinz were forbidden to learn English. She said we rarely spoke actual words to each other because of this and that it was especially hard because I was so inquisitive.

I asked her, "Why did they do this?"

She said it was for security. My parents could talk English in front of them when they needed to say something in secret. In turn, because I was so curious, they needed me to not understand German so when their agents came to the house, I wouldn't know what they were talking about.

Wow! I began thinking of Tanta's hands and how I never heard her talk. Same with Sisi and Heinz. How hard this must have been for them and for me! No wonder I struggled learning German in college. I had been in a non-verbal relationship for the first seven years of my life!

Sisi went on to tell me about my father John's frequent trips to Berlin, and how long and dangerous they were. Each time he left she feared he wouldn't come back. She remembered a time when my father traveled to Russia. Beyond that, she didn't know anything else.

I began to wonder if she knew anything about my birth mother Karin. I asked her if she did.

She thought for a minute and then recalled a time when Gertrude hired a lawyer named Werner Hammerschmitt to meet with Karin in jail. He was the one who was able to finally get Karin to sign the adoption papers. She said I was ten months old by then.

Wait!! Werner Hammerschmitt??

That's the name I saw in the book of Faust!

My mind wondered if Karin gave that book to Werner to give to Gertrude as part of the agreement. Indeed, Gertrude had sold her soul to the devil by forcing Karin's hand and keeping all of this a secret.

I could feel my anxiety rise as I realized once again the depth of information that Gertrude had withheld from me and from Sisi. How could she have done what she did? How could she say that my mother was a no-good drunken prostitute, when she herself forced the adoption?

It seemed that I was reliving the same heartbreak that my mother Karin felt when she realized her mother had betrayed her. Why did this all have to happen like this?

Why couldn't Sisi and I have had the past 50 years together? I would have learned German from her. She would have learned English from me.

But that had been taken away from both of us.

The way she was looking at me was clearly the way a mother looks at her child. I was now 57 years old and she was 85. The pain was becoming unbearable as we realized that we each had to take advantage of the time we had now.

My heart was pounding, as I let them both know the real reason why I had come.

I said, "Sisi, I came to see you to let you know how much I love you and Heinz, and how much I have missed you. Whatever happened that split us apart doesn't matter anymore. All I care about is that we are together now."

She nodded in agreement, but I could see she was also clearly upset. The person she had so admired, my mother Gertrude, had also betrayed her. That fact was finally settling into her reality as she sunk deeply into her chair.

I sensed the anger, betrayal and confusion within her, I realized that she now felt the same way I did, the same way Karin did and possibly the same way Gertrude did.

I knew I was here to help Sisi let go of her sadness by giving her the gift of unconditional love.

It was such a bittersweet and powerful time for both of us. We were finally together again and I wanted to enjoy every moment we had.

"What sort of child was I?" I asked, trying to shift the focus onto something more playful.

"You were always very independent and smart. Your mother Mrs. Virtues pushed you a lot more than she pushed Henry."

Then she smiled at me with a twinkle in her eyes and said, "Did you know that you named me Sisi, and that my real name is Julianna?" I was stunned.

"Because you called me Sisi that became my name. You named Tanta, too. I never knew Tanta's real name."

She was grinning from ear to ear because she loved the fact that I named her Sisi and that it has been her name ever since.

Suddenly Sisi stood up and said, "Come, let's take a walk to our favorite café for coffee and torte."

As we walked the short distance to the café, I could feel the love between us with every step. The café was charming and featured a large display case filled with German pastries, *kuchen*, tortes and cakes. I felt like a child, peering through the rounded glass case trying to decide which to eat. I wanted all of them. I chose an almond cake layered with hazelnut and chocolate buttercream.

We sat at a small white circular table in the corner opposite the window.

The sun was shining through the window as the waitress poured hot coffee into each of our cups. The smells and sounds of this little café were intoxicating. I had imagined sharing moments like this for years and now it was real. By the time our cakes arrived I was already satisfied. Every bite was an extra treasure.

As we finished, Sisi leaned over and whispered into Sabine's ear. After a serious and lengthy conversation, Sabine looked at me and said, "Sisi wants to see you again, but she is worried that you won't be able to talk to each other. I have to work the rest of the week and she is only comfortable seeing you during the day."

I asked Sabine to comfort Sisi by reminding her that if we understood each other when I was a little girl, we should be able to understand each other now.

As Sabine said this, I saw the relief on Sisi's face.

I suggested that we could go to the Palmengarten, near Holzhausen Park and eat lunch in their wonderful cafe. As Sabine relayed this piece of information Sisi nodded in agreement and smiled at me.

"Sisi wants to spend the entire day with you, but it will only be her. Heinz will stay home," Sabine announced.

I could feel that we were both relieved, excited and a bit nervous at the same time. I knew that if we didn't do this, we would regret it for the rest of our lives. It was so comforting to not have to say good-bye to Sisi right now.

When I awoke that Monday morning, I was so grateful to be alive. I swung open the window in my hotel room and felt the warmth of the sun mixed with the crisp breeze of autumn. I could smell the scent of fall leaves, coffee and fresh bakery floating through the air. The sound of the S-Bahn, Frankfurt's mass transit system, rumbled beneath me.

My heart was happy as I walked to meet Sisi.

As soon as she saw me, she said in very broken English, "Laural, not want Palmengarten."

I asked, "Sisi, do you not want to go?"

She shook her head no and said, "Sisi take you shoppen for coat."

I smiled, "You want to take me shopping for a coat?"

I could see her face beaming with pride and relief, as I felt the anticipation rise within me.

I was thrilled with the idea; this would make everything so much easier as we were already standing in the middle of the Zeil, Frankfurt's premier shopping district. My heart grew warm just thinking of the adventure that was ahead, and the joy of being alone together for an entire day.

Sisi surprised me with a gift. She pulled out a little brown stuffed bear and handed it to me. "For you, Laural, a bear, talisman," Sisi said.

My mind raced. Does she know that bear is my animal guide? I graciously accepted it and brought it to my heart and said, "*Danke*. Yes, bear is talisman for Laural."

217

She then smiled and put her hands to her heart and said, "Bear, talisman for Sisi!"

Wow, we are both bear people! I hugged her like a bear and she hugged me back. I could feel her heart sink into mine as our bodies relaxed and we became one. From that moment on, the language barrier did not exist.

We walked arm in arm down the street, beaming inside. We would glance at each other and giggle or smile. I could tell she was very, very happy and so was I. This was exactly what we both needed, some time to really feel and honor the heart connection that existed between us.

Eventually we walked into a department store and I began trying on coats.

She would shake her head yes or no as I tried on different coats. I found one fairly quickly that felt right. It was a long dark chocolate brown wool coat with pockets and a hood. It had velvet trim around the cuffs and in the back.

We both loved it but this was the first shop we walked in. Neither of us wanted to commit this soon. That would take the fun of the adventure out of the day.

We left the store and I tried on coats in at least three other department stores. Then we ate lunch and had a real conversation.

It was amazing how much we could actually say to each other with our limited vocabulary. There were a few times when we stumbled, but today was about sharing love. It wasn't about the big questions and heavy answers.

Sisi standing next to a stuffed bear in the store where she bought my coat. - 2012

218

It was about Sisi and me finally being together. It was what we had both dreamed of for the past fifty years. After lunch we found a store with a big bear in it so I took a photo of Sisi hugging the bear. We really enjoyed the fact that we both loved bears so much. We looked in a few more stores and then Sisi decided we should go back to the first store and buy the brown coat with the hood. I was so happy. I knew every time I would put it on I would remember this day. That coat was my bear coat from Sisi. Each time I wore it, I would feel hugged by her. We were both clearly very happy with our decision.

I wanted to show Sisi my mesa and see if she would understand what it meant to me.

I brought her up to my tiny hotel room. I was hoping that if she understood the concept of a talisman, then she might understand this. I held my mesa to my chest and said, "Mesa, talisman."

Sisi pointed to my chest and nodded "yes?"

I began to open it; I could see she was fascinated. After I had it fully unwrapped, I placed my stones in a circle. Again, she was mesmerized.

I then picked up the stone that represented Gertrude and held it in my hand to show her, and said, "Mrs. Virtues."

Sisi pointed to the stone, "Ahhh Mrs. Virtues."

Yes, she understood!

Then I set it back in my mesa and picked up my father John's stone and said, "Mr. Virtues."

She smiled and looked at me. "Yes, Mr. Virtues."

I went on and showed her each stone one at a time, letting her know what they meant. Karin, Lonnie, Paul, Tyler, Holzhausen Park. She would nod and smile after each one as if she were honoring them. I remembered that I had taken a stone from Lake Michigan out of my mesa the night before and set it on the windowsill with some chestnuts.

It was a green and pink stone I had picked up along the beach in Algoma last summer. I remembered falling in love with that stone and thinking how unique it was. It was very much a stone from the heart. When I realized it was for Sisi, I handed it to her and said, "Algoma."

She clutched her chest and gasped, "Algoma?"

I said, "Yes, Algoma, for you, Sisi."

I placed the stone into her outstretched hands. She brought it to her heart and muttered the word "Algoma" several times, as if she were anchoring this stone into her soul. She looked up at me with tears in her eyes and smiled. She nodded as she accepted my gift to her.

I sensed she understood how this stone represented all the years that she and I were separated and how this stone will now be a reminder that would keep us together.

As we sat there looking at each other, I placed my hands over her hands as she held the stone over her heart.

I said, "Algoma, Sisi and Laural, together."

She nodded in agreement and then she began speaking German really fast.

I knew that Nikos, the young man working at the front desk, could speak Russian, English and German.

"Sisi, *sprechen Sie Deutsch*?" I asked gesturing with my hands that we should go downstairs to the front desk. She immediately was speaking in German and I could see he was trying to take it all in so he could tell me everything she was saying. Then she stopped and he turned to look at me.

"She said she wants you to know that she understands what your stones mean; that she collects stones and Heinz thinks she is crazy. But she is not crazy. She has collected stones since she was a child and puts very special ones on her dresser in her bedroom. She wants you to know that she has a special stone from the Baltic Sea. The stone you just gave her is now the most important stone she has."

I thanked Nikos as Sisi nodded in agreement, beaming from ear to ear. I hugged her and thought what a miracle this day had been. It was as if all the heartache and years apart had just dissolved in that single moment.

Everything she needed to know about me was held in that stone. It held the truth that our souls had always been together. Our physical bodies may have been on different sides of the Atlantic Ocean, but the love in our hearts was never separated. She accepted my gift as a touchstone to our lives and our love.

We walked out of the hotel to find a café to have some coffee and *kuchen*. We ended up going to the same place where we had lunch. I sensed Sisi liked routine and this was comfortable for her. As we sat there, we looked like two Cheshire cats grinning at each other.

I could also feel the mother bear in her, and I sensed she could feel it in me, too. All the years of confusion seemed to disappear as only love remained.

When the moment came for us to part that evening, I gently touched her face with my left hand.

I said, *"Ich liebe dich,"* I love you.

Tears reached out from my heart to hers as the train drove out of sight.

On my final day, I went back to Holzhausen Park to thank it once again for holding a part of my soul so sweetly for all these years. The sun was shining and the trees seemed to be dancing in the sunlight. The leaves created a spectacular canopy of color. This was one of the warmest days during my trip. It was liberating to be walking around in sandals in late October. I knew this would be my last day here, at least for now, so I drank in every bit of it.

I walked to the far side of the park and treated myself to an old-fashioned Holzhausen picnic lunch.

I bought an authentic frankfurter from the parks outside café with brown mustard and dark German bread, plus a glass of apple juice. My mind flashed to my childhood and how Sisi and I would do this exact thing when I was young.

I sat back and listened to the sounds of children playing in the park as well as adults sitting at the café tables enjoying lunch and talking with their friends. I belonged here, in this park, in Frankfurt. It all felt so natural and comfortable to me, as if I had never left. I thought of all of my adventures on this trip and how magical it was.

I walked to the space I had been visiting and opened my mesa once again. I wanted to integrate the healing work I had just done with Sisi and my soul, as well as the tree and the land it lived on. I thanked all of the trees for holding space for me during my life and on this trip.

It felt so right to be sharing this work with this magical place that I loved so dearly. The stones within my mesa seemed to be silently singing along with the birds and enjoying the sun as much as I was.

After several hours of expressing my eternal gratitude for everything this park represented, I knew it was time for me to go home to the United States. I closed my mesa once again, and strolled down the Avenue of Chestnuts to retrace my steps to the house of my childhood.

Life was good and I was blessed to be here.

CHAPTER 22: THE RETURN

As another fall was beginning to descend into our lives, I received an unexpected email from Sabine. She had just visited Sisi and Heinz at their home and learned that Sisi had fallen, broken her leg and had surgery. During their visit Sisi began crying, expressing concern that she would never see me again. As I read Sabine's words I could feel my heart aching to return to Frankfurt as soon as possible.

It was now October 2014, and I would be turning 60 in December. I understood the trepidation that comes after surgery for I had had two full knee replacements in the past three years, my right knee in 2011 and then the left in 2013.

I immediately made plans to leave on November 27, and return December 8. Sabine confirmed that she could be with me to translate. I talked with Paul about the possibility of me staying longer if they needed my help, and he understood. I wanted Sisi and Heinz to know that if they needed me, I would be there for them, just as a daughter would be there for her parents.

I started imagining how wonderful it would be to celebrate my birthday with all of them and to enjoy the holidays and the *Christkindlmarkt* together. I shared my itinerary with Sabine before I purchased my tickets and made hotel reservations. A few days later Sabine replied that Sisi was thrilled to hear that I was coming and that those dates worked perfectly. My heart filled with anticipation as I made the final arrangements. Just the thought of being with Sisi on my birthday was a dream come true.

I could feel the little girl within me excited to go home and be with them.

On the morning of November 3, I sent my final itinerary to Sabine. Later that day I saw an email from Sabine in my inbox. I opened it and read the words, "Dear Laural, I'm so sorry to tell you this, but Sisi passed away last night in the hospital."

My heart froze in absolute disbelief as tears began streaming down my face. Thoughts swirled like dried leaves in the wind as I tried to catch my breath. How could this be happening now?

Later that night Sabine and I talked on the phone. She explained that Heinz had called her to let her know that Sisi was gone. He was devastated and wanted Sabine to let me know so I could change my plans, which I didn't. When I asked Sabine what happened, she said that Sisi had suffered a brain bleed and the only option she had was surgery. According to Heinz, the surgery would have left her in a wheelchair, potentially blind and deaf. Sisi chose to not have the surgery and died later that night.

November 11th was Sisi's memorial service. She had pre-arranged to be cremated and buried in the Südfriedhof Wiesbaden Cemetery. I had asked Sabine to bring two bundles of six white roses for me, and to place one bundle on Sisi's grave and give the other one to Heinz. Sabine also brought two white lilies to honor Sisi.

Sabine emailed several images to me during the service. One was the brass urn that held Sisi's remains, the other showed the gravesite with our flowers on the frosty yet freshly tilled earth. These were the only flowers that marked Sisi's final resting place. Heinz held a single red carnation that he gently set on Sisi's urn as it was lowered into the ground. I was so grateful to Sabine for being in my life and for attending the service. She was my lifeline during this difficult time, who shared my love for Sisi with Heinz.

As I silently packed my suitcase, I realized that this wasn't the trip I had planned, but I sensed it was the trip I needed. Ten days of reflection would be good for my soul.

A damp breeze greeted me as I stepped out of the taxi onto the worn cobblestone streets of Frankfurt's medieval city center. The smell of grilled sausage and hot mulled wine (*Glühwein*) filled the cool air while the Christmas Market (*Christkindlmarkt*) spilled onto the streets in front of me. Hundreds of little wooden shops decorated with lights lined the pathway to my hotel, which was in the middle of these festivities on a pedestrian street. The sound of my luggage tugged at my heart as it rumbled over the cobblestones reminding me that I was now in the city where I was born.

Hotel Neue Kramer is a narrow five-story boutique hotel. A large plate glass door with a brass handle marked its entrance. Inside a shiny marble-lined hallway led to a cramped two-person elevator. I picked up my keys on the second floor before going to my room on the fifth floor. When I opened the door a dozen blood-orange roses and red holly greeted me. They were a welcome sight and a stark contrast to the tiny white room that was mine.

I opened the envelope and read its message, "Welcome home, I will see you soon! Love Sabine."

Eventually I walked out onto the streets and blended into the crowds. We seemed to move as one weaving through the sensory experience of the market. Everything I had been looking forward to now felt very surreal. When I stumbled upon an open-air farmers' market I was grounded by the scent of fresh apples, squash, cheese and freshly baked bread. A diminutive and weathered farmer was sitting next to a table filled with handmade wreaths. I bought a small evergreen wreath to place on Sisi's grave. It was my way to share the holiday season with her.

I tried to reach Hazel that night. I was hoping to visit with her and see the inside of the house again. I had called several times from the States and now again with no answer. I had my laptop with me so I searched for her online. Within moments I found myself reading her obituary! Hazel had died on November 9th, exactly seven days after Sisi. I sat on my bed absolutely stunned by this bizarre turn of events. Both Rolph and Hazel were gone. My dream of standing in my childhood home once again was over as well.

The next morning I stood at the end of the street waiting for Sabine to arrive. In front of me was a traffic jam filled with cars beeping and honking but going nowhere. I saw a large produce truck wedged into a narrow road. When Sabine pulled up on the sidewalk in a tiny rental car, I jumped in as quickly as I could. I sat quietly as Sabine drove backwards for three blocks. An elderly lady yelled at us that we were going the wrong way. Once we were free from the congestion we could breathe, we looked at each other and began laughing at the scene we left behind.

When Sabine turned onto the Autobahn toward Wiesbaden, I began to focus on the fact that I was actually sitting next to her. Sabine's strength and beauty struck me; she was now a sophisticated woman working as a human resources manager for an international law firm. As she drove, she told me about her boyfriend and how she often walks by my old house because he lives near Holzhausen Park. I told her about Hazel and Rolph. She wasn't surprised because it had seemed empty for a while now.

We both surmised that Hazel may have been ill, and in the hospital before she died. Since they had no heirs Rolph and Hazel had set up a trust worth 25 million Euros for the Frankfurt International School they helped to create in 1961. How fortunate I was to meet them and share stories.

I do wish we would have had more time together, I sensed they would have had more insights into my life, but now I would never know if that was true.

Sabine said that the house would be sold for millions because it stood on one of the most prized pieces of real estate in Frankfurt. This wasn't a surprise for I knew it's historical and architectural significance. Plus, its proximity to Frankfurt's city center and Holzhausen Park made it an ideal location.

As I reflected on how priceless that home was to me, memories of my enchanted childhood flooded my mind.

Sabine turned off the autobahn to Wiesbaden and we headed straight to the cemetery. It was then that Sabine said Heinz was not feeling well and was home waiting for us, so we would be visiting Sisi's grave on our own. This news pierced my heart and a wall of tears spilled forth.

A cold mist hugged the air as we walked under the ancient stone arch that marked the entrance into Wiesbaden's palatial garden cemetery. It took a while to find Sisi's grave. The scene was something out of Alice in Wonderland meets the Adams Family. When we reached her gravesite, we saw that our flowers were literally frozen in time. It looked like a still life portrait capturing the exact moment when Sabine placed them on the earth three weeks ago. I set the cedar wreath near the base of the flowers and pulled a stone from my pocket. It was a piece of chain coral from Lake Michigan, with two small holes shaped like hearts that formed an infinity symbol. I set it into the center of the wreath and honored the woman who had loved me forever and had never given up on finding me.

Heinz was clearly in pain when we arrived. He was relieved to see us. Hunched over, he grabbed his lower back and motioned for us to sit in the living room. The house was immaculate and silent.

We sat while he recounted the events of Sisi's last days, releasing the burden of the grief he was carrying alone. He said that she had fainted in the bathroom and that he pulled out his back trying to pick her up.

He called the ambulance and they took her to the hospital. It was here that they performed a series of tests and discovered that her brain was hemorrhaging and her only option was surgery. When they told Sisi that the surgery was risky and that it would leave her in a wheelchair with no guarantees, Sisi said, "No."

"I'm so sorry Laural that Sisi isn't here for you." Heinz cried, as he explained how they gave her some pain medication and that she died in her sleep during the night. He clutched my hand and I placed my hand on his heart.

"I am here for you because I love you just as I love Sisi," I said through the tears.

He nodded and told me how they were married the exact year I was born and how he saw me on the day I was brought into the Virtues family. I was surprised because I thought they were married when I was four. He said that I was remembering the time when they began living with us. It was then that I saw my little girl in his eyes. He was not looking at the 60-year-old woman I had become, but the child who was like a daughter to him.

In that moment Heinz decided to take us to the neighborhood café for coffee and kuchen. As we walked this now familiar route, I clung onto him like a doting daughter. Tears of love and grief flowed between us and into each other's arms.

When we returned, Heinz wanted me to choose something special to remember Sisi. When he opened her closet doors, I immediately felt Sisi's essence as her scent filled the room. A stuffed bear immediately caught my eye. Heinz handed me the bear and said his name was Timo.

He smiled as he patted the bear on the head and knew that I would love it just as Sisi did. He warmly placed both hands over mine as he gave me two of her scarves.

Heinz said he was now very tired and needed to nap. We gently hugged each other and said our goodbyes.

On my 60th birthday I awoke to the sound of doves and church bells. By now I had become accustomed to my daily ritual of strolling through the streets and markets, stopping to enjoy a latte macchiato, and watching people of all ages bustle about. But today was different. Today was the reason I had chosen to be here, to celebrate my life and to reconnect with my childhood. Even though Sisi wasn't here as I had planned, this day was for me to embrace the wonder of the little girl that lived within me.

I pulled open the dark wooden door and brushed back the opulent red velvet drapes to reveal the intimate and Baroque dining room of Zarges. This was an established restaurant that transported me back in time. I was fortunate to have a seat near the front window looking out onto the Zeil. This was the perfect place to reflect on my life and watch the myriad of people walking by. In my heart I was hoping someone would notice that I was an American and talk to me in English. My waitress seemed uninterested and too busy to strike up a conversation. She was cordial in guiding me through the menu as I chose pumpkin soup and a salad with honey thyme dressing.

I found myself staring out the window at men in suits carrying briefcases, fancy ladies with fur coats and high heels, plus people of all ages bundled up for holiday shopping. I saw young couples in love, friends enjoying a simple day together, families sightseeing and busy people on singular missions.

Every once in a while, someone would stroll up to the window to read the menu or gaze at the artful pastries in the bakery next door. I indulged my imagination in the reality that my home was only five blocks away. I drifted through time and saw myself living in our villa with my parents and imagined coming here on a regular basis.

When my waitress placed my bowl of pumpkin soup topped with toasted pumpkin seeds drizzled in pumpkin seed oil in front of me, I wished she had asked me why I was here so I could tell her. But, she didn't.

"*Danke*," I said, with anticipation.

"*Bitte*," she replied, distantly distracted.

As I savored every spoonful of this decadent soup, I remembered eating soup in the kitchen with my mother Gertrude and Sisi. Soup was always a mainstay in our home and I learned at an early age how to eat it like a lady.

My mind began playing out the scenario of why I wished someone would ask me why I was here. Was it so I could say I was celebrating my 60th birthday and that I was born here and I was wanting to feel recognized? As my need to be recognized and relevant entered my mind I realized that no one cared, and why should they? Everyone had busy lives and stories to tell. Why was mine any different?

I sat with that thought of wanting to belong as I broke off a piece of crusty bread and soaked up the last drops of soup. Seamlessly an exquisite salad was placed in front of me and the empty bowl was whisked away. As I gazed into this masterpiece of a salad, I saw how fortunate I was to be able to give myself this gift.

No one needed to know who I was or why I was here; it was only I who needed to know that I belonged here. I sunk into my chair and settled into my thoughts.

The salad was everything I had hoped for.

The taste of honey and thyme mixed together with white balsamic vinegar was sweet and satisfying. I sipped the latte macchiato in front of me and life was good.

After lunch I walked next door to Zarges Bakery. Here were rows of the most luscious pastries and tortes imaginable, each a work of art. I chose three that were placed in a fancy pink and black box tied with cotton string. This box held my birthday cakes and I could not have been more pleased. I strolled quietly back to my hotel to enjoy a little of each in the privacy of my room.

That afternoon I revisited the outdoor stalls of the Christmas Market and sampled a skewer of dried fruit dipped in dark chocolate. I bought a few more gifts for Tyler, Maya and Paul.

I heard a choir of young people singing German holiday songs mixed in with the music of the carousel's pipe organ. I walked into a woodcutter's shop and marveled at the intricate handmade ornaments. There were fanciful wooden mushrooms with dotted red caps and ladybugs reminiscent of my childhood.

I bought a pair of mushroom ornaments plus a carved wooden sun and moon to bring home.

As night came, hundreds of local people spilled into the narrow streets to drink mugs of hot mulled wine.

Tonight, I was celebrating my birthday with Sabine. Since I saw her on Sunday, she had flown to London and back for work and just this morning she took a train to Koln. Sabine made a special trip back to Frankfurt to celebrate with me, knowing that she would have to travel back to Koln the next morning. I marveled at her tenacity as she rode her bike from the train station to meet me at Café Nizza.

Café Nizza is an upscale restaurant overlooking the Main River. We had chosen it together because we both loved their fruit and goat cheese salad.

She had reserved a window seat and we talked for hours about life, love and her new career. Sabine didn't think Heinz was up for a visit this next Sunday, so she invited me to Bad Hömburg Castle and its outdoor market as her birthday present to me.

With great love and affection, we hugged goodbye. She rode away on her bike and I walked through the sights and sounds of the Christmas Market to my hotel room.

I rose the following morning ready to revisit Holzhausen Park once again and to see my old home. Peering through the gate I could see that the house was now shuttered and empty. I also noticed several large cracks in the foundation. It still looked magnificent as I said goodbye to yet another cherished member of my family. I thanked the house for all it had given to me, my family, Sisi and Heinz and of course Hazel and Rolph.

I walked to Holzhausen Park and was shocked to see that only three of the old oaks were still standing. The earth looked barren and raw. As I approached the singular grand old oak standing in the middle of the park, I noticed a young man sitting on one end of the circular bench surrounding it. I sat on the other side, so not to disturb him. Tears quietly rolled down my face as I realized I was saying goodbye to this entire part of my life.

"Halo," the young man said, standing in front of me.

"Hello," I replied, pleasantly surprised.

"Oh, you are American," he said excitedly.

"Yes, I am, so you speak English?" I asked.

"Yes, and you love the trees here, too?" he asked.

"Yes," I nodded with an inquisitive almost bewildered smile. This seemed too good to be true.

"Are you from here?" he questioned.

"I lived here till I was almost seven. I had a special tree that lived here, too," I replied with anticipation.

"Where was it?" he asked curiously.

"Right over there." I pointed to the exact spot.

"Oh, I remember that tree and the day ten years ago when that tree fell down. I came to the park for my daily walk and it was broken and bent over like a bridge." He used his arm to replicate how it looked bent at the elbow. "There was a thunderstorm the night before so I think the tree was hit by lightning and the wind blew it down," he explained.

"After that, the other trees began to fall until the park officials realized that something was wrong. This past year they tested all the old trees and cut down the ones that were not healthy. They planted new ones in their place," he said, motioning to the saplings nearby.

I was stunned as I realized he was recapitulating the last day of my tree's life with me just as Heinz had done for Sisi. Hearing this directly from someone who knew the tree I loved so dearly was a miracle. I couldn't imagine a more perfect gift for my birthday.

"The old trees are making room for the parent trees so their children and grandchildren have room to grow." As I spoke those words, I felt its message deep within me.

A wave of gratitude and deep peace flowed through me as grief continued to nudge in my heart. The cycle of life and death were now giving birth to a new perspective.

We introduced ourselves to each other and I thanked Nikolai for sharing his story. We shook hands and he gave me his email so we could write to each other. He said he was excited to have an American friend.

As he walked away, I found myself in a place of powerful peace. In that moment I saw everything as a gift and how fortunate I was to be alive and to be right here now.

I reflected on all the years I had wondered and questioned as well as my sorrow and heartbreak. By giving myself permission to go into the depths of my wounds I was able to feel authentic joy.

Rays of sunlight streamed through the gray clouds as I said goodbye to the park and walked the worn cobblestone streets back to Frankfurt's city center.

I received a message from Sabine at the hotel that Heinz wanted to see me on Sunday before I left. I was looking forward to visiting the castle and market in Bad Hömburg, but I was way more thrilled to see Heinz again.

Sabine greeted me in the same tiny rental car she had before. The drive to Wiesbaden seemed to fly by, and before we knew it we were parking on the side of a steep hill outside Heinz's upstairs flat. Heinz was waiting for us at the top of the steps and quickly motioned us into his home. His face seemed more relaxed and he was in less pain. We sat in the living room as he pulled out a simple blue box. He emptied its contents onto the living room table in front of us.

Out tumbled Sisi's jewelry, a collection of beaded necklaces, bracelets and rings. Her taste was simple and earthy. Beyond the mounds of pearls and chokers was a beautiful amber ring set in solid gold. I sensed it might be the most valuable of her possessions. As I slid it on my finger I knew it was not for me. I gently pulled it off and handed it to Sabine.

"This ring isn't for me, it is for you," I said.

"Don't you want it?" Sabine asked.

"It's not that I don't want it; it's that I want you to have it. It's a gift for bringing me home to Sisi and Heinz and all that we have shared the past ten years," I answered.

"It's beautiful, what is it made of?" Sabine asked.

"Baltic amber," I replied with a smile. Heinz smiled knowingly as Sabine slipped the ring onto her finger.

"What is amber?" Sabine inquired.

"It's fossilized tree resin that is millions of years old and now it is with you," I answered.

She smiled, as she understood the significance of this ring and how it held the ancient essence of trees in the timeless form of the sacred circle.

I left Frankfurt the next morning feeling blessed.

As for my special purpose...

I now understood that I have been living it every day of my life.

"Trees are sanctuaries.
Whoever knows how to speak to them,
whoever knows how to listen to them,
can learn the truth.
They do not preach learning and precepts,
they preach undeterred by particulars,
the ancient law of life."
- Hermann Hesse -

EPILOGUE: THE REFLECTION

When I returned from Frankfurt in December 2014, I could sense this chapter of my life had come to a close. My focus shifted to our life in Green Bay and our son Tyler. He was now living in Williams, Oregon with his life partner Maya. He was teaching at Hawthorn Institute, an herbalism and ayurvedic school he created. Paul and I began traveling to Oregon to help them manifest their dream.

I was continuing to teach yearlong medicine wheel intensives along with mandala classes and retreats, including a class on ancestral healing. I was inspired to take another DNA test, this time with 23&me. DNA testing had evolved dramatically since 2007 and I wanted to know more.

When I received my results, I discovered that my maternal Haplogroup was now defined as K1b2a, which represents an ancient Indo-European lineage connected with the Bell Beaker culture of Europe. I asked my biological brother Lonnie to also do a DNA test to see if we could discover more about our paternal lineage. As it turns out we are primarily French/German, Scottish, English and Irish.

Our combined autosomal DNA also showed that in the 1700's we had distant grandparents who were each 100% African (Angola, Nigeria & Congo), Native American, Ashkenazi, Egyptian and Portuguese. This revelation was fascinating but not surprising. I had always suspected that my birth father's colonial roots were complex.

I could only imagine all the stories they held.

My biggest mystery was still my maternal grandparents, Johann and Henrietta. I was told by my mother that her father was a Sephardic Jew who left Germany in 1938. I was able to find Karin's birth certificate, which revealed that Johann was born in Solingen-Höhscheid, Germany, but there were no other records of him. I was unable to find any evidence that tied Henrietta with the Nazi Party. What I did discover was that they had both been incarcerated by the Gestapo in Frankfurt sometime after 1934, which was fascinating and confusing. I tried to obtain their marriage certificate from the records department in Frankfurt, hoping it would name Johann's parents, but they wouldn't give it to me because Henrietta was still alive! I tried to explain that she had died in 1994 in Turkey, but because they didn't have a death certificate on file; they had no proof. I reasoned with them that if she were still alive, she would be 104! That didn't seem to make a difference.

Regardless of the lies and betrayal Henrietta had inflicted on Karin, she at least tried to fix it by risking her life to find me. As conflicted as she was, she is the one who set out to find me and made it possible for me to find Karin before it was too late.

I'm grateful that John and Gertrude created such detailed binders of their years of service in Frankfurt. If they hadn't kept such detailed records, I wouldn't have any proof of their time working with the CIC and CIA.

Obviously finding Sisi and Heinz was a gift that provided me with the confirmation and closure I needed. They validated so many aspects of what had happened to us before we left Germany. Meeting them gave me some sense of peace with not having the answers to all of my questions.

Clearly World War I & II as well as the Cold War represented a precarious and dangerous period in time for everyone living in Europe, especially Germany. The level of scarcity, secrecy and trauma caused many to keep their stories to themselves.

Writing this story while trying to untangle a giant web of secrets was both challenging and freeing. It gave me a way to feel connected to each of my parents, even though they weren't physically with me.

I began writing this book in 1994 when this journey of self-discovery was ignited by Karin's dream of having our story told. It took me 15 years to write and publish the first version, which I titled *The Tree Oracle* in 2009.

In 2012 I added more chapters and republished it as *The Guardian Tree*. When I returned from Frankfurt in 2014, I chose to officially end my story after Sisi's death.

I loved our home in Green Bay, which had become my teaching space. I was now facilitating a seventh, one-year medicine wheel that began in 2015 and would end in November 2016.

As it turned out 2016 was a pivotal year for us all.

Tyler and Maya were married on February 12, on the island of Kauai. The day before we left to fly to Kauai, Paul was told that the company he worked for (Jag Outdoor Advertising) was being sold to an investment group. He had been with them for twenty-five years as vice president. We weren't sure what the future held for us at this point.

During this same time, I was deepening my study of the Andean cosmology by learning from Peruvian Altomisayoq Adolfo Ttito Condori (Tupaq Ttito Kuntur) as well as Ana Larramendi and Teri Nehring. Both Ana and Teri travel extensively with Adolfo in Peru as they facilitate group trips with him to the sacred mountains. I was never able to go because of my knee replacement surgeries. My ability to hike in high altitude was definitely limited. During one of those trips with Teri, Adolfo expressed interest in facilitating a series of classes at my home in Green Bay. I was thrilled to host Adolfo and his brother Rodolfo (T'ito Q'osnipa Kuntur) in August for a series of intensive classes. Each class filled up rapidly with 20 – 30 students each. Fortunately, Teri, Ana, Adolfo, Rodolfo and I, along with our friend Margie, were able to carve out one magical day for an outing to Algoma and Lake Michigan. It was surreal to have Adolfo sit with me under the exact trees of my childhood. He honored the sadness I felt there as a child. He asked me what my dreams were now. I told him that Paul and I were beginning to dream of moving to Oregon and living near Tyler and Maya. Adolfo encouraged me to follow my vision, for I had finished my work in this place.

Jag Outdoor officially became Link Outdoor several months later. Paul was let go without a severance package, he was 64 and I was 62. We moved to Oregon that same month and found ourselves applying for Social Security and government healthcare much earlier than we had planned.

We live a much simpler life here in Southwestern Oregon. Paul spends his time painting and fishing on the Rogue River. I continue writing. It was here that I began to create a tarot book based on trees, titled Tree Spirit Tarot.

In February 2019 we were blessed with the birth of our grandson Kai. In October 2024 we welcomed the birth of our granddaughter Hazel. This was so much more than I ever imagined.

We were exactly where we were meant to be.

Currently I'm co-creating a series of children's books titled the <u>Everlasting Forest</u> with Lanvi T. Nguyen. I also continue to write articles for my blog Tree Spirit Wisdom. Both give me the opportunity to combine my love of trees with the joy of being a continual wonderer.

My most recent project has been to create a family tree for Kai and Hazel, going back seven generations for both Tyler and Maya. My wish for them is to always know how loved they are and to know their roots.

"The true meaning of life is to plant trees,
under whose shade you do not expect to sit."
- Nelson Henderson -

APPENDIX

This story naturally divided itself into twenty-two chapters that reflect the twenty-two aspects of the Major Arcana in the Tarot. As I connected to the Tree of Life, I realized I had walked the archetypal journey of the heroine.

<u>**Comparison of chapters to the Major Arcana of the**</u>
Chapter 1: The Fairy Tale - **Fool** - Innocence, zest to learn...
Chapter 2: The Message -**Magician** - Heavenly Father
Chapter 3: The Separation - **High Priestess** - Heavenly Mother
Chapter 4: The Confusion - **Empress** - Earthly Mother
Chapter 5: Letting Go - **Emperor** - Earthly Father
Chapter 6: Moving On - **Hierophant** - Education
Chapter 7: Starting Over - **Lovers** - Decision
Chapter 8: The Secret - **Chariot** - Freedom
Chapter 9: The Impossible - **Strength** - Helpful Guides
Chapter 10: The Tree of Life - **The Hermit** - One's True Nature
Chapter 11: The Shift - **Wheel of Fortune** - The Calling
Chapter 12: The Preparation - **Justice** - Maturation
Chapter 13: The Reunion - **Hanged Man** - The Anticipation
Chapter 14: The Start - **Death** - Facing Fears
Chapter 15: The Release - **Temperance** - Guide of the Soul
Chapter 16: The Wonder - **Devil** - Acknowledging your Shadow
Chapter 17: The Roots - **Tower** - Death & Rebirth
Chapter 18: The Insights - **Star** - Inspiration
Chapter 19: Full Circle - **Moon** - Mysterious Rebirth
Chapter 20: My Awakening - **Sun** - Return to the Light
Chapter 21: Coming Home - **Judgment** - Healing
Chapter 22: The Return - **The World** - Innocence Renewed

"Into the forest I go
to lose my mind
and find my soul."
- John Muir -

ACKNOWLEDGEMENTS

I wish to thank everyone who has supported me on this heroine's journey and those who have read the countless versions of this living diary I call a book. It has taken me over twenty-five years of dedicated writing and research to release this story to the world. Each and every page was a journey that challenged me to see my life through new eyes. Some of what I saw was difficult to write, but my heart knew I needed to continue. Through this never-ending process I found the inner peace that sustains me to this day.

I dedicate this book to my parents: Gertrude and John, Karin and Lonnie as well as Sisi and Heinz for everything they sacrificed. They are the silent heroes I hoped to acknowledge by telling our story with truth and integrity. This story hasn't been easy to expose, for each of them lived in a world of secrets that were held so close that lives were constantly in danger. But it is time.

I thank all of my grandparents for holding space for me as I tried to heal this ancestral pattern for seven generations forward and back. I especially thank Henrietta and her determination to not give up on finding me, regardless of the consequences. She gave me the opportunity to face my deepest fear, heal my life and learn what true compassion and forgiveness is.

I am grateful for my brother Henry and my siblings Viola, Lonnie and Caroline, as well as my half-sisters Phyliss and Lonnie.

I am grateful for the support of Paul's entire family as we lived out this story in real time.

I will forever cherish Rich Bonkowski who continually encouraged me to find my birth mother until I did. My gratitude goes to Bill Hanley for taking my first 100 pages of hand-written notes and typing them into a computer so I could build upon it and give to my mother before she died. I treasure John Lewis for believing that this story could become a movie and sending it to Dreamworks when it was still only a dream. Maybe someday it will. My heart aches for David Lerman, a man of amazing grace, who passed away shortly after we reunited in 2012.

I wish to honor my forever-friend Debbie, who never tired of proofreading each and every revision and has been my biggest cheerleader. I thank Karla Giraldez for helping me refocus and to Becky Lerner for providing the vision to turn this into a reality. Plus, I thank Jean Wentz and Irmine Hero for sitting with me as I worked through my feelings. And to Barb and Steve Prust, for giving me the final push.

I want to thank Sandy Van Sistine for telling me what my name Carmen Sylvia meant and the little lady who told me stories about my mother Gertrude. I am grateful for the never-ending support of Gertrude's best friend Ethel Zimmerman for cheering me on as I found the courage to share my story in Algoma for the first time.

To Kim Klein Dorchester for taking such beautiful photos of me that made my heart shine, and Anne Bronsveld for her thoughtful cover design.

I am blessed with so many amazing women in my life: Debbie, Teri, Holly, Bonnie, Maya, Alyona, Chris, Lisa, Carol, Tanya, Ellen, Jean, Karen, Ruth, Marcia, Teri, Jenny, Rose, Rosie, Lana, Sally, Joellyn, Patty, Kate and Janet to name just a few. You have helped me sort through the tears and emotions as I uncovered more pieces to the puzzle.

To Betsy and her amazing daughter Leah for gifting me the print of Holzhausen Park.

I want to thank Jan Bogren for lending me her camcorder so I could capture the magic of Holzhausen Park. I am forever changed because of the teachers in my life: Judith Cornell/Rajita Sivananda, Ana Larramendi, Adolfo Ttito Condori, Teri Nehring, Mary Raymakers, Jamee Curtis, Linda Fitch and Lynn Berryhill etc. Each of you provided me with the guidance and support necessary to heal my heart and rewrite my story.

My heart expands in infinite gratitude to my husband Paul who has supported me as I left the financial security of my career to pursue my passion. He had to live with weeks, months and years of me obsessing over my computer and talking through my emotions. Listening to me retelling my story a thousand times until I could understand what I was truly feeling. I could not have done this without your support on so many levels. My mother Karin was right: you are my soul mate and you are my rock. I love you dearly.

To my sweet and amazing son Tyler who has walked this walk with me and kept me grounded every step of the way. You are the inspiration I needed to heal this story for you, your children and grandchildren. Your wisdom and steadfastness helped me to see what you saw all along. You are wise beyond your years and I am grateful that your soul chose me as your mother. I am thankful that Maya joined our lives and held space for me to complete these final chapters.

I have given this story to the universe in hopes that my grandchildren will feel empowered to know the secrets of their grandma's life and the infinite love I have for them.

Finally, I wish to thank Sabine, my German angel on Earth. You entered my life like a miracle and tirelessly translated as Sisi, Heinz and I tried to piece this puzzle of a life together. Without you, I would not have been able to understand what had happened and who was waiting for me.

I love you all.

"The Tree of Life lives within each of us,
helping us awaken to our true nature.
Let us reach out with branches of compassion,
connect with each other through our shared roots,
and hold space for all to grow and feel loved."
- Laural Virtues Wauters -

RESOURCES

Andrews, Ted. (1993) *Animal Speak*. Woodbury, Minnesota: Llewellyn Publications.

Andrews, Ted. (2004) *Nature Speak*. Jackson, Tennessee: Dragonhawk Publishing.

Banzhaf, Hajo & Theler, Brigitte. (2000) *Tarot and the Journey of the Hero*: Samuel Webster; Red Wheel/Weiser.

Cornell, Judith. (2006) *MANDALA: Luminous Symbols for Healing*. Adyar, India: Quest Books, Theosophical Publishing.

Ingerman, Sandra. (1997) *Soul Retrieval: Mending the Fragmented Self*: New York, New York, Harper One.

Ingerman, Sandra & Wesselman, Hank. (2010) *Awakening to the spirit world: the shamanic path of direct revelation*: Boulder, Colorado, Sounds True, Inc.

Jung, C. G. (1968) *Man and his Symbols*: New York, Dell.

Sams, Jamie. (1999) *Dancing the Dream - The seven sacred paths of human transformation:* San Francisco, HarperCollins.

Villoldo, Alberto. (2000) *Shaman, Healer, Sage*: New York, New York, Harmony Books.

9 780615 534596